HARMONY ON THE PALATE

MATCHING SIMPLE RECIPES TO EVERYDAY WINE STYLES

Shari Darling

THE SOPHISTICATED WINO

whitecap

Edited by Lori Burwash

Proofread by Viola Funk

Design by Janine Vangool

Illustrations by Jacqui Thomas

Front cover image by Edward Pond

Back cover image by Steve Livingston

Food Styling by Chef Brian Henry and Joan Ttooulias

Photographs by Rob Kinghorn

Printed and bound in Canada

Library and Archives Canada Cataloguing in Publication

Darling, Shari

    Harmony on the palate : matching simple recipes to everyday wine styles / Shari Darling.

Includes index.

ISBN 1-55285-701-8

    1. Cookery. 2. Wine and wine making. I. Title.

TP548.D37 2005   641.5   C2005-903040-2

The publisher acknowledges the financial support of the Government of Canada through the Book Publishing Industry Development Program for our publishing activities.

Images courtesy Wine Institute of California, Australian Wine Export Council, Steve Livingston, Niko Coutroulis, Argentina Winery, Altavista (the Argentina Wine Company), Premium Port Wines, Dairy Farmers of Canada

CONTENTS

I dedicate this book to Hazel Legge (29 April 1948 to 11 July 2005), in loving memory of her laughter and friendship and magnificent meatballs.

ACKNOWLEDGMENTS

Special thanks to my teammates, AnnMarie MacKinnon (publishing coordinator at Whitecap) and Lori Burwash (my editor), for their enthusiasm, commitment, vision, expertise and support for my book.

It wouldn't have been possible for me to write this cookbook without the generosity of spirit, artistic influence and scientific expertise of the following experts. To you all, thank you:

Linda Bartoshuk, PhD — Research Scientist, Otolaryngology, Yale University School of Medicine

Mary Evely — Chef/Instructor, Santa Rosa Junior College Culinary Center and University of California, Davis, Extension Program. Mary is also a wine and food affinity consultant to wineries and restaurants in California.

Landmark Education Corporation Forum Leaders, Jack Schropp (my husband) and the volunteers for their ongoing contribution to my life

Isabelle Lesschaeve, PhD — Director, Cool Climate Oenology and Viticulture Institute, Brock University, Ontario

James Manners — Winemaker, Inniskillin Wines

Ann Noble — Professor Emerita, Enology, Department of Viticulture and Enology, University of California, Davis. Creator of the wine aroma wheel and consultant

Cathy Ruggieri-Davidson — Product Consultant, Liquor Control Board of Ontario

Finally, special thanks to all who willingly tested my recipes to ensure they worked for a second and third time, as well as giving your feedback on the wine style accompaniments. Your generous contributions, support and teamship allow me to stand behind this work with confidence. I appreciate all of you. Thank you.

Jen Bird, Betsy Brown, Pat Brownscombe, Les and Brenda Bulgin, Debbie Crossen, Rod Davidson, Rheba Estante, Michael Gravelle, Brenda Lachance, Michelle LeDuc, Larry Patterson, Sue Pulfer, Linda Robinson, Cathy Ruggieri-Davidson, Phil Spearman, Khadija Sunderji, Frances Wdowczyk

INTRODUCTION

Sipping a glass of wine while eating is always enjoyable. But when you focus your senses of sight, smell and taste on how flavors dance and harmonize on your palate and share this experience with those around you, the moment takes on greater meaning. Dining is transformed into an expression of living in the moment.

The wonderment and magic of our senses draws so many of us to the world of wine and food. Every person experiences this magic individually. There are as many interpretations of wine and food pairing as there are people. Every person's interpretation is valid.

This cookbook expresses my unique interpretation. My discoveries are no more or less valid than yours. Perhaps the only difference between us is that I have turned my passion for wine and food into a living as a writer. In doing so, I've learned the language of wine and food so that I can share my passion, exploration and discoveries with you.

Wine and food pairing is often expressed as an art form. I find that viewing this magical world from both a scientific and artistic perspective enriches my own experiences and understanding of wine and food. After all, scientists and artists aren't all that different. Both work with ideas that are first shaped by the imagination. Similarly, pairing wine with food is a creative process that blends structure with chance.

With the influx of immigrants into North America, our culinary world continually embraces new ethnic dishes, cooking techniques and exotic ingredients. This is especially the case in Canada — many of us embrace multiculturalism as our culinary identity.

With all these new flavors, successfully pairing wine with food is a risky business, even for those working within the culinary industry. To complicate matters, often we are told that certain wine and food partnerships work well together, without being told why. One wine expert suggested that white wines generally work well with runny cheeses. Why? Or, a general guideline I've seen suggested countless times is to drink white wine before red. Why? These emphatic statements have been followed blindly for decades without anyone questioning them. As a result, they create more confusion than joy for many people, including me.

I began to wonder if there's a simple, consistent approach to successfully and frequently matching wine to any ethnic cuisine. Through research, interviews and plenty of serious drinking and eating — important experiments, I must add — I came up with a system of three simple principles you can use for creating harmony on the palate. I refer to these as the Building Block Principles.

The Building Block Principles aren't a new set of guidelines. In fact, I'm sure the ideas have been around for as long as wine has existed. Until now, however, wine and food experts and lovers have used these ideas sporadically, subjectively or intuitively. Many wine and food consumers may not be using them at all.

I approach wine and food pairing systematically, using the Building Block Principles as a way of thinking about how and why certain wines work with specific dishes. I've used this system time and again in my wine certificate programs, with restaurant management teams and in client appreciation events. It's a system everyone can learn and remember.

HOW THIS COOKBOOK WORKS

This book is for foodies who focus on a dish before choosing a matching wine, but also for winos, like me, who search for recipes to pair with one's favorite vintages. Regardless of how you choose wine and food pairings, the Building Block Principles will work for you.

Part 1 reviews the scientific and artistic expressions of pairing wine with food to create harmony on the palate. In Part 1, you'll discover—

- *the role that taste and flavor play in our enjoyment of wine with food*
- *how to build a solid foundation between wine and food*
- *how to create a flavor design for your wine and food partnerships*
- *how to harmonize flavors using the Harmony Charts at the beginning of each chapter in Part 2*
- *how to taste wine*
- *how to read and rework, if necessary, recipes for pairing success*

Part 2 consists of the recipes and suggested wine notes. Since wine style is an important element to consider in creating harmony on the palate, the recipes are organized into chapters highlighting a variety of popular wine styles. Some chapters contain more recipes than others. My aim wasn't to keep the chapters equal but to pick recipes for their simplicity, tastes and flavors, as well as their ability to work with specific wine styles.

WINE STYLES

Wine styles derive from the interplay of many elements, such as the geography, climate and soil of a particular region or vineyard, the grape variety or varieties grown and vinified, and winemaking techniques. I haven't covered all the styles that are paired with food and certainly not all wine styles in general. For instance, I've refrained from including sherry, madeira or other fortified wines. I'm probably as big a wino as there is, but even I don't drink these fortified wines on a daily basis. They're fabulous wines, don't get me wrong.

My objective is to include the main wine styles people are most likely to drink and consider with meals on a daily basis. After all, the recipes are simple, easy to prepare and designed for everyday consumption. The wine styles covered are sparkling; crisp, dry white; medium-bodied white; big, fat white; off-dry white; off-dry rosé; light, fruity red; red with forward fruit character; austere red; late harvest and icewine; and Port and port-style.

Organizing the recipes by wine styles makes it easy for you to find foods that pair well with wines you enjoy or have in your cellar. It may also broaden your horizons. Every wine style consists of an array of wines produced from around the world. This organization shows the wide range of international wines that fall within a specific type. So you can stick with the kinds of wines you like, or you can experiment with other wines in the same style. For instance, if you prefer the tart, refreshing acidity of a crisp, dry Sauvignon Blanc, you may want to try a Vinho Verde from Portugal, knowing it shares the same qualities. For those one-of-a-kind vintages still sleeping in the wine cellar, you need only look at their building blocks to know what wine style they fall under. Once you have the wine style, you can then find the ideal food match to make the most of these special vintages.

RECIPES

In each chapter, you'll find recipes for such items as appetizers, soups, salads, pastas, chicken and red meat dishes. The recipes come from a variety of sources. While I developed many from scratch, others are renditions of my favorite restaurant dishes or cherished recipes from my earlier cookbooks, now out of print but given new life here. A few special recipes come from friends who are avid cooks, talented chefs and diehard wine lovers.

Regardless of the dish and the source, simplicity is the theme. After all, I'm not a chef. The recipes use as few ingredients as possible, which can usually be found in your local supermarket. The trick is to hunt for local, fresh and quality ingredients to maximize on colors, textures and flavors. For cooks like me, the easier the recipe, the greater the opportunity to create a masterpiece. You'll notice, however, a trend toward ethnic, hot and spicy foods.

WINE NOTES

A two-part wine note accompanies each recipe. The first part explains the predominant building blocks in the wine that work with the predominant building blocks in the food. The second part focuses on creating a flavor design for harmony between the recipe and the wine. Use the notes as a guide for incorporating the Building Block Principles into your decision-making. You'll very quickly gain confidence in choosing wines for yourself.

THE SCIENTIFIC ART OF WINE AND FOOD PAIRING

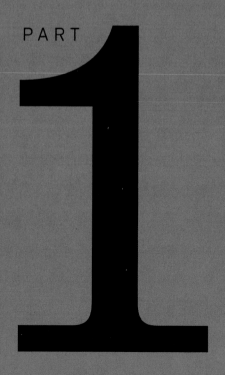

1

EXPLORING THE SCIENCE OF OUR **SENSES**

Our senses help us survive. They're also the source of our pleasures. When it comes to enjoying wine and food, we primarily use our senses of taste, smell and sight.

The anterior part of our tongue, the part that wiggles when we move it, comprises nerve systems. When we drink, chew and swallow, these nerve systems produce two types of sensations that work together to create our drinking and eating experience: taste sensations and flavor sensations.

TASTE SENSATIONS

The Chorda tympani branch of the facial nerve carries our sensations of taste. We're born with a natural and instinctive ability to distinguish four basic tastes for survival — sourness, sweetness, bitterness and saltiness.

SOURNESS

We still don't fully understand the ability to distinguish sourness, although it's believed to be related to primitive membrane sensitivity to potentially harmful acids. The attraction to sourness shows up in a love of lemons or a craving on a hot summer day for the sourness of a chilled, crisp, dry white wine. Sourness comes from the acidity in wine and food.

SWEETNESS

We're born with an instinctive love of sweetness. We appreciate the sweetness in fresh fruit, honey and chocolate, to name a few. Sweetness is also a taste some people desire in wine.

BITTERNESS

Our natural ability to distinguish bitterness helps us avoid poisons. Many bitter substances are harmful, especially when consumed to excess. Yet we're also attracted to bitterness. Many people enjoy the bitterness of walnuts and in austere, full-bodied red wines.

SALTINESS

Our nerves and muscles require salt to function. Severe salt depletion would kill, so we've evolved to seek out salt when we need it. We crave the saltiness of a wide variety of ingredients and foods, such as cheese, potato chips, peanuts, sunflower seeds, raw oysters and smoked salmon.

FLAVOR SENSATIONS

Flavor sensations include the taste sensations (sourness, sweetness, bitterness, saltiness) plus two other groups: the trigeminal and retro-nasal sensations. These groups include the flavors of spiciness, fruitiness and fattiness.

TRIGEMINAL NERVE SENSATIONS

The trigeminal nerve is responsible for the sensations of pain and burn, touch and temperature that can assault our mouth, and that we detect as warning signs of a variety of potentially harmful stimuli.

As well, the trigeminal nerve allows us to experience the positive effects of chemosensory irritations in beverages and foods. The spiciness or pleasant pain and burn of cayenne, the effervescence of champagne and the carbonation in soda aren't tastes, but chemosensory irritations — flavors — that many people enjoy and crave.

RETRO-NASAL OLFACTION SENSATIONS

The trigeminal input helps the brain determine whether an odor came into the nasal cavity via the nose (ortho-nasal) or mouth (retro-nasal).

Retro-nasal olfaction is the perception of odors from inside the mouth. When we chew and swallow foods, the odors produced are forced behind the palate up into the nasal cavity.

Born neutral to odors, we learn to like or dislike them based on our experiences and their effect on us. We enjoy certain foods because of the odors experienced from inside our mouth, such as the fruitiness in fresh fruit. We also enjoy the odor and mouthfeel of butter, olive oil and other fatty ingredients. On a negative note, if a food or beverage once made you sick to your stomach, it may smell disgusting to you for the rest of your life.

UMAMI

Umami, meaning "yummy" in Japanese, is considered by many to be a legitimate fifth taste sensation in Asian cuisine. It's naturally present in protein-rich foods such as cheese, meat, fish and human milk. It can also be distinguished in seaweed, soy sauce, fish sauce, green tea, sardines, fresh tomatoes, cooked potatoes, peas and fermented beans. Even though most North Americans have no idea what umami is, it's an integral element in our diet, experienced as savory, that most people love.

Controversy still exists as to whether umami should be considered when pairing wine with food. After all, North American palates don't recognize umami specifically because we've never been taught to identify it. Some wine and food researchers say umami can be detected in wines that have reached a state of perfection in their gentle balance of flavor, maturity and quality. This state is believed to be achieved only through the aging of wine for three to ten years in the wine cellar.

The term used by some to describe wines possessing umami is "slow wines." Slow wines are said to be the ideal match for foods naturally rich in glutamate, the substance responsible for umami, such as cheese and aged beef, or those cooked slowly for a long time, such as braised beef or vegetables. Long, slow cooking causes the breakdown of proteins in the food, releasing their natural glutamate and contributing to their umami or savory flavor.

Other experts believe that umami isn't a fifth taste sensation but a combination of the tastes sweet and salty, and is therefore non-existent.

CHAPTER 2

WHAT KIND OF **TASTER** ARE YOU?

Taste buds are sensory organs on the tongue that allow us to experience tastes. Our sensory sensations differ according to the number and distribution of our taste buds. In addition, everyone produces a varying amount of saliva, and at a different rate, which also affects perception of taste.

Dr. Linda Bartoshuk is a professor in the ear, nose and throat section of the surgery department at the Yale University School of Medicine. She conducts research into genetic variations in taste perception, oral pain and taste disorders. Dr. Bartoshuk says people are born with a genetically determined number of taste buds and divides them into three groups, according to the number of taste buds they have. "Super-tasters" account for about 25% of the population, medium-tasters about 50% and non-tasters 25%.

According to Dr. Bartoshuk, super-tasters possess more taste buds than medium- or non-tasters. As a result, they experience the taste, temperature and texture of foods, most specifically bitterness, more keenly than medium-tasters or non-tasters. To the super-taster, espresso, olives, arugula, dark chocolate and dry wines can taste too bitter and are therefore not palatable. Super-tasters experience intense tastes and oral burns from chemical irritants such as chili peppers, black pepper and cayenne. They also perceive the most intense sensations from salt, acids and sweeteners, as well as fats in foods.

For years, my parents have been playfully arguing over who is the better cook. My mother is a super-taster. She lightly salts her foods, uses a minimal amount of garlic and refrains from spicy foods altogether. My father is a non-taster, as am I. We tend to overspice and like pungent blue cheese, strong coffee, spicy foods, anchovies and cured olives. I also add lots of garlic to my recipes.

SUPER-TASTER'S TONGUE   **NON-TASTER'S TONGUE**

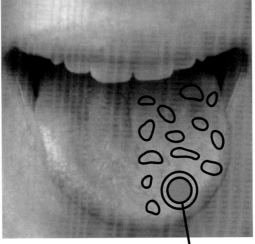

Notice the difference in the number, size and shape of taste buds between a super-taster's tongue (left) and a non-taster's (right).

Fungiform Papillae
papillae are smaller and
closely arranged

Fungiform Papillae
fewer, larger papillae
more loosely arranged

Are you a super-taster, medium-taster or non-taster? Why not test yourself? You'll need a cotton swab, polyvinyl ring (used for reinforcing punched holes in binder paper), blue food coloring, a mirror and a magnifying glass. Place the ring on your tongue near the front, not on the tip. Using the cotton swab, put a tiny drop of food coloring inside the ring.

Use the mirror to look at your tongue through the magnifying glass. Pink dots will emerge through the blue dye. The dots are fungiform papillae, mushroom-shaped structures containing taste buds. If you have more than 35 dots in that area, you're a super-taster. If you have 15 to 35, you're a medium-taster. Fewer than 10 makes you a non-taster.

Knowing that there are different kinds of tasters can help you choose foods and accompanying wines for your guests. Future dinner parties may now include a variety of delicate and bold wines and foods for your super-, medium- and non-taster friends.

THE TONGUE MAP

Many wine books include a generic diagram of the tongue map, showing where the sensations of sourness, sweetness, bitterness and saltiness are experienced. Such diagrams give the impression that the taste sensations are experienced in discrete, defined areas on our tongue.

This tongue map was derived from a map published in 1901 by D.P. Hanig. Hanig believed that if the thresholds for acid, sweet, bitter and salty could be shown to vary differentially around the tongue's perimeter, this would support his thesis that these taste sensations have distinct physiological mechanisms.

Here's what my tongue map looks like:

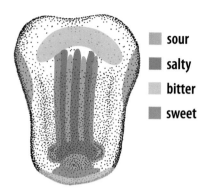

- sour
- salty
- bitter
- sweet

However, scientists have found Hanig's map to be misleading. Some believe it was improperly translated into English upon arriving in North America. Others believe that the idea that taste sensations are experienced in localized areas on the tongue is based on dated research and now incorrect. In fact, new research shows that taste sensations aren't necessarily confined to specific areas.

The accuracy of this generic map is unimportant as it has little practical use. What *is* useful is to know that the regions of the tongue and the ability to perceive tastes and flavors differ enormously between people.

Where do *you* experience sensations? You can discover this by creating your own tongue map. Draw a tongue on a piece of paper, and keep your pencil handy. Next, gather citric acid (lemon juice), sugar, bitters or tonic water and salt. Place each sample in a dipping cup or bowl and dilute with a half teaspoon of water. Using a small, clean paintbrush, paint an area of your tongue with each solution, starting with the sugar solution. While the tip of the tongue is sensitive to sweetness, you'll most likely be able to perceive aspects of this sensation in other regions. Mark where you perceived each taste on your tongue map.

Although most taste buds are on the tongue's edges, with relatively few down the center, my tongue map shows that I experience little, if any, sensation on the edges. Dr. Bartoshuk explains that this lack of sensation is likely due to taste damage, which is very common (even a cold can damage taste nerves). As a non-taster, I assault and no doubt damage my tongue by regularly consuming lots of hot sauce and raw garlic. Fortunately, the taste system is built with a lot of redundancy, so even when parts of it are damaged, whole mouth taste stays relatively constant.

Whether you work in the wine and food industry or are just a wine and food lover, it's helpful to be able to identify sensations and where you perceive them and to study the relationship between them. The more you understand about your own tongue, the better your ability to understand how a wine was built in its grape-growing and winemaking stages and whether its building blocks and flavors harmonize. As well, understanding your own palate helps you immensely in understanding how tastes and flavors in wine and food ultimately work together.

CHAPTER 3

THE BUILDING BLOCK PRINCIPLES

While we may all perceive tastes and flavors at varying intensities, most people can recognize and immediately identify certain predominant sensations.

Certain tastes and flavors can be the source of wine and food trends. Heavily oaked Chardonnay was once a preferred wine style. Today, it takes a back seat to other emerging wine styles. Trends in ethnic foods exist as well. Thai food became a trend about a decade ago and is still popular today. Indian curry was once considered exotic. Today, most supermarkets carry a wide range of hot and spicy international curries.

Certain ingredients are also quickly identified. Most of us can recognize the taste and flavor of butter, the sweetness of chocolate, the bitterness of walnuts and the saltiness of peanuts. It's these quickly identified and familiar tastes and flavors that are considered when pairing wine with food.

By first considering these tangible and familiar tastes and flavors, you increase your chance of successfully pairing the right wine with a dish to create harmony on the palate.

These tangible and familiar tastes and flavors are the building blocks of wine and food. More importantly, these predominant building blocks play a major role in how wine and food partnerships either harmonize or clash.

BUILD A STURDY FOUNDATION

Building a harmonious wine and food partnership is like building a house. First, you build a sturdy foundation on which the house can sit. The building blocks that go into a house's foundation are tangible materials, such as cement, brick, wood and nails. A wine and food partnership can be as sturdy as a house if its foundation is similarly built with tangible, predominant building blocks.

The recognizable tastes and flavors forming the Building Block Principles, as well as some basic examples, are the following:

- *Sourness (lemon, vinaigrettes)*
- *Sweetness (chocolate)*
- *Bitterness (radicchio, cured olives, walnuts)*
- *Saltiness (fresh oysters, capers, anchovies, smoked salmon)*
- *Fattiness (butter, cream)*
- *The hot and spicy (black pepper, cayenne, chilies)*
- *Fruitiness (blackberries, apricots)*

Often, one or a couple of these flavors predominates in a certain ingredient or dish.

Wine also possesses tangible building blocks, just not as many as food. These building blocks work together to form each style of wine. The building blocks for wine are:

- *Sourness (acidity)*
- *Fruitiness (fruity aromas and flavors)*
- *Sweetness (residual sugar)*
- *Fattiness (buttery aromas and flavors, oily mouthfeel and creamy texture)*
- *Bitterness and astringency (tannin)*

So how do we partner the building blocks in wine with those in food to create a solid foundation?

THE FIRST PRINCIPLE: MATCH SIMILAR BUILDING BLOCKS

Match the most predominant building blocks in the wine to the same ones found in the food — pair sweetness with sweetness, sourness with sourness, and so on.

No dish or wine style consists of only one building block. However, the most predominant building blocks are the ones to consider first when looking for a food partner. Pairing similar, predominant building blocks creates a bridge of compatibility between the wine and the food. Here are a few basic examples:

- *Sourness with sourness — the acidity in a vinaigrette with the crisp acidity in a crisp, dry white wine*
- *Sweetness with sweetness — the sweetness of chocolate with the sweetness of a dessert wine, such as Port*
- *Fattiness with fattiness — the fattiness in butter with the oily mouthfeel and creamy texture of a barrel-fermented or aged white wine*

THE SECOND PRINCIPLE: OFFSET DISSIMILAR BUILDING BLOCKS

Offset building blocks only when absolutely necessary. It's necessary when the food has certain building blocks that don't exist in wine. For example, some foods are salty, spicy or hot and spicy, but no wine style possesses these building blocks. Therefore, saltiness and hot and spiciness must be offset by building blocks that do exist in wine, such as sourness and sweetness. Offset the saltiness in food with the sourness in wine — pair fresh raw oysters with a crisp, dry white wine. Offset hot and spicy flavors in food with sweetness in wine — pair Thai chili pepper with an off-dry wine.

THE THIRD PRINCIPLE: MAKE SURE THE WINE'S PREDOMINANT BUILDING BLOCK IS MORE PRONOUNCED THAN THE FOOD'S

Some food and wine pairing authorities say wine shouldn't dominate food and food shouldn't dominate wine; a perfect balance is necessary. This certainly makes sense — theoretically. But without being able to sample most wines before purchasing them, how do you create this perfect balance on a consistent basis?

The answer is that you can't — unless, of course, you're a sommelier, wine importer or winemaker regularly tasting wines. Add to this that wine is a living, changing organism, aging in the wine cellar. What may be a perfect balance of sensations in the wine and food today may not necessarily create balance five years or even a year later.

Nonetheless, harmony on the palate *can* be achieved on a consistent basis without having to strive for perfection. This is accomplished by following the third principle: make sure the wine's predominant building blocks are more pronounced than the food's. This applies to both the pairing of similar or offsetting of dissimilar building blocks. For instance, a wine should offer more bitterness than the bitterness in food. Or a wine's sweetness should be greater than the hot and spicy flavor in food.

When the wine's building blocks are more pronounced, you can be sure the partnership will work. On the other hand, if you allow the food's building blocks to dominate, the wine's character will be diminished, if not entirely lost, and the partnership will most certainly be imbalanced.

How do you know which wines possess specific predominant building blocks? Choose wine, not by its producer, region or grape variety, but by its wine style.

THE IMPORTANCE OF THINKING WINE STYLES

Wine styles are determined by their combined building blocks. Here are the most predominant building blocks in each wine style.

To choose dishes accordingly, think in terms of wine style first, considering the predominant building blocks in your favorite vintage. Or distinguish the predominant building blocks in your favorite dish and pick a wine style to match. The Building Block Principles work for both foodies and winos!

The good news is that every wine style offers an array of grape varieties and wines from all over the world. At the beginning of each chapter in Part 2, I've listed a wide range of international wines for that particular style. The list helps you distinguish your favorite building blocks in wine and in food and then explore the tastes and flavors of the world.

WINE STYLE	SOURNESS	FRUITINESS	SWEETNESS	FATTINESS	BITTERNESS
Dry sparkling	•	•			
Off-dry and sweet sparkling	•	•	Some		
Crisp, dry white	•	•			
Well-balanced, medium-bodied, smooth white	•	•		Some	
Big, fat white	Some	Some		•	
Off-dry white	•	•	Some		
Off-dry rosé	•	•	Some		
Light, fruity red	•	•			
Red with forward fruit character	Some	•		•	Some
Austere red	Some	Some		•	•
Late harvest and icewine	•	•	•		
Dry Port and port-style	•	•			
Sweet Port and port-style		•	•		

A CLOSER LOOK AT THE BUILDING BLOCKS

SOURNESS

Sourness is a taste sensation and an important ingredient in foods such as vinaigrettes and citrus fruit. It's also the sensation perceived on the palate from the level of acidity found in a wine. Acidity gives wine its refreshing lift and crispness. Our palate perceives a wine's acidity for about four to eight seconds, depending on the type, level of acidity and an individual's threshold.

The old rule says that vinegar and wine are enemies. This isn't necessarily true. It depends on the strength of the sourness in the vinegar and the wine chosen as a match. Pair the sourness in a vinaigrette with the sourness in a crisp, dry white wine. Just make sure the wine has more acidity than the vinaigrette. For example, white vinegar is more acidic than wine, making it an offensive ingredient to match to wine. Balsamic and rice

vinegars, however, are sweeter, allowing the wine to be more sour than the vinaigrette.

Fresh lemon, while having sourness as its predominant building block, still has some fruitiness and a hint of natural sweetness. Lemon vinaigrettes are highly compatible with a wide range of crisp, dry white wines. Why? Because crisp, dry white wine is more sour than the sourness in lemon. Grilled or deep-fried calamari doused in fresh lemon juice paired with a sour, crisp, dry white wine most certainly offers harmony on the palate.

On the other hand, if you pair a food with sourness with an austere red with heavy tannin, it will only make the wine taste more bitter. This is because the sourness in the food overpowers the natural soft acidity in the red wine. As a result, what's left in the red wine is a one-dimensional and predominantly bitter taste.

To create a harmonious partnership when matching the sourness of wine to saltiness in food, make sure the wine's sourness is greater. If the dish is too salty, your crisp, dry white will taste flat and nondescript and lose its fruit character.

SWEETNESS

Sweetness is a taste sensation we're born to love. The sweetness in wine makes the flavors more concentrated. The greater the sweetness in the wine, the more mouthfeel, or tactile sensation, perceived.

Sweet foods can cause crisp, dry wines to taste dull, as our perception of the fruitiness is lost. Sweet foods will also cause austere red wines to taste too bitter, while making sour wines taste more sour.

When pairing sweet wine to a food with sweetness, make sure the wine is sweeter. If the dish is sweeter, the wine will taste flat or too tart, even if its sugar level is high. The good news is that you can rework recipes, such as desserts, to be less sweet, so they work well with sweet wine.

When pairing a sweet wine with a hot and spicy dish, apply the third Building Block Principle — make sure the wine's sweetness is greater than the hot and spicy flavors in the dish. I once made a cold pasta salad with a Thai chili sauce. The dish paired wonderfully with an off-dry Riesling because the wine's fruitiness and sweetness were greater than the pasta's spiciness.

Two days later, I used the leftover sauce to make the same dish. But because the chili had been marinating for 48 hours, the sauce was twice as hot and spicy, overpowering the fruitiness and sweetness of the Riesling. It took the more intense fruitiness and sweetness of a late harvest wine to dominate the hot and spicy flavors in the sauce.

BITTERNESS AND ASTRINGENCY

Bitterness and astringency both come from tannin in wine, but are different sensations. Bitterness is a taste sensation, while astringency is a mouthfeel — flavor sensation — that creates a puckering or dryness. They work together as the building block of bitterness in their relationship to food.

Tannin gives wine its aging potential in the wine cellar, as well as adding structure and body to wine. It comes from many sources, including the grape skins and stems extracted during pressing or maceration, when the grape juice is left in the vat in contact with the grape skin and stems. It also comes from the oak barrels used to ferment and age wines. French oak barrels seem to impart more bitterness to wines than American or East European oak.

If a wine has too much bitterness, it may be unsuitable for any food. Some wines are meant to be stored in the wine cellar until the tannin can precipitate over time and soften some of the bitterness, bringing the wine into balance.

Bitterness is found in a variety of foods, including walnuts, spinach, radicchio, cured olives and fresh herbs, such as oregano, thyme and rosemary. These ingredients, when incorporated into a dish, offer bitterness but allow the wine's bitterness to predominate. Dishes highlighting sourness or sweetness mostly clash with the building block of bitterness in wine.

SALTINESS

Saltiness contrasts nicely with sourness in wine, yet it can increase the perception of alcohol in wine. That's why it's important to make sure the sourness in the wine is greater than the saltiness in the dish.

In the introduction, I referred to an expert's suggestion that white wines generally work well with runny cheeses and asked, "Why?"

The reason is the salt. Cheese is high in salt because salt is used to halt fermentation during the cheese-making process. A white wine's sourness contrasts with cheese's saltiness, making wine and cheese the most well-known contrasting yet harmonious partnership. Other salty foods that work well with high-acid white wines are smoked salmon or fresh oysters.

Salty foods can also work well with reds, in particular reducing the bitterness in red wines high in tannin. The saltiness in food tends to soften the bitterness in the wine. If you choose an austere red wine as a partner because you enjoy the bitterness, keep the salt content in the food to a minimum. Otherwise, the wine's best feature will be thwarted. If the wine's bitterness is too great, use more salt in the dish.

FATTINESS

We often hear that we should marry the weight of the wine with the weight of the food. This guideline deals mostly with the building block of fattiness. Fattiness is experienced on our palate as chemosensory and retro-nasal sensations. It adds weight to both wine and food and is one of the flavors that most people can quickly identify.

Fattiness is a tangible and important building block in wine, especially wines from hot climactic regions, where grapes attain high sugar levels, which means greater alcohol content. This high alcohol gives wine an oily or fatty mouthfeel. In these regions, red and some white wines may be put through a secondary malolactic fermentation. This process converts some of the wine's tart malic acid to softer, creamier lactic acid. Malo-conversion also produces diacetyl, which gives white wines the characteristic

odor and mouthfeel of real butter. Reds with heavy alcohol and tannin — fattiness and bitterness — fall into the austere red wine style.

Fattiness is present in a variety of oils (olive, vegetable, sesame, peanut), butter and cream. It's also a building block in animal and poultry fat and in oily fish, such as salmon. Fatty ingredients, such as butter and cream, harmonize with wines possessing the same weight — big, fat whites. Austere reds work well with red meat, oil-based pasta, oily salmon and high-fat gravies. Sourness in food clashes with the fattiness and bitterness in austere reds. In fact, the combination has been described as metallic and offensive.

HOT AND SPICY

The hot and spicy is a flavor — a chemosensory irritation — and a tangible building block to be considered when pairing wine with food. With the influx of multiculturalism into North America's culinary world, hot and spicy flavor is easily identifiable in a wide range of dishes.

Sweetness in wine nicely offsets hot and spicy foods. When we eat hot and spicy food, our mouth is numbed. What survives is the ability to taste sweet and sour. Therefore, match hot and spicy foods to wines with sweetness and some sourness. These building blocks are found in off-dry white or off-dry rosé wines. Austere reds increase the perception of heat in our mouth, so it's best to avoid those. Off-dry rosés are the only red wines that work with hot and spicy food, due to their sweetness.

FRUITINESS

Fruitiness is both a flavor experienced through ortho-nasal and retro-nasal olfaction and a building block in wine and food. Because the flavors and aromas of fruity wines are often confused, fruitiness needs more attention than other building blocks. Wines are often described as having a sweet, fruity aroma, when they actually possess a ripe, fruity aroma. Wines can smell like ripe fruit, but they can only taste like sweet fruit. Sweetness is a taste sensation only experienced on the palate. This confusion has led many wine and food lovers to match dry table wines possessing deliciously ripe fruit aromas and flavors to dishes containing sweet fruit.

A classic example is the pairing of a dry Chardonnay, with its ripe apple character, to sweet applesauce and pork chops. The wine's acidity tastes unpleasantly sour when paired with the sweetness in applesauce. An off-dry white wine with some sweetness, despite its flavors, is a better match.

To attain the fruity character in wine, various techniques are used. Trellising ensures that grapes get plenty of sunshine, bringing out their fruit flavors. Fermentation and aging in oak barrels also helps mellow the herbal and grassy tones of Sauvignon Blanc, bringing out the fruit flavors. In the production of reds with forward fruitiness, such as Zinfandel, a few different winemaking techniques are employed, such as less skin contact during fermentation to keep the tannin soft and a malolactic conversion to reduce the acidity.

These techniques allow the fruitiness of the wine to shine bright and match a variety of foods. For example, the sourness and fruitiness of lemon juice drizzled over fillet of sole harmonizes with the sour and lemony flavor of a crisp, dry white, such as Sauvignon Blanc. Roasted tomatoes and roasted beets both lose their acidity and gain a concentration of fruitiness that matches fruit-forward reds, such as Zinfandel or Merlot.

FRUIT WINES VS. FRUITINESS IN WINES

There's a difference between fruit being used to make wine — fruit wine — and the building block called fruitiness. Wines made from fresh fruit, such as peaches, pears, apples or berries, are a particular wine style that can also possess the building blocks of sourness, bitterness and sweetness.

Table wines made from grapes, however, can have aromas and flavors that resemble a wide range of fruits, even though that fruit isn't actually in the wine. So, an apple wine made from apples is supposed to smell and taste like apples. Table wines produced from grapes, such as Chardonnay, may possess aromas and flavors reminiscent of fresh apples, but these characteristics are more subjective.

CELEBRATING THE ART OF WINE WITH **FOOD**

Once you've constructed a solid foundation of tangible building blocks using the Building Block Principles, you can think in terms of the partnership's flavor design. It's time to set science aside and make room for your artistic expression!

FLAVOR DESIGN

The flavor design of your wine and food partnership includes the use of your sight, smell and taste. Flavors are experienced as one's creative expression and are highly individual. Two people can smell and taste the same wine and come up with two completely different flavor profiles.

Compusense is a sensory technology company, a world leader in computerized sensory analysis offering the only technology of its kind in the world for food. Among their many agendas, Compusense has partnered with Inno Vinum, a wine-sensory strategy

company owned by Isabelle Lesschaeve, a wine-sensory specialist. The partnership now brings sensory technology to the wine world. Lesschaeve helps wineries establish flavor profiles for their wines. This allows wine-makers to blend artistic expression with the scientifically proven taste demands of wine consumers.

I attended a Compusense workshop in which a group of eighteen people blind tasted a variety of wines, including a Chilean Sauvignon Blanc. I was the only taster who worked in the wine industry. Having a frame of reference for wine in general and for this particular varietal wine, I guessed the wine accurately as being a Sauvignon Blanc and described the flavors as grassy and grapefruit-like, the flavors commonly attributed to Sauvignon Blancs.

Having no experience in wine, the others had no perceived frame of reference for the flavors of this particular grape variety. As a result, they described the wine as having flavors of peach, raspberry, melon, apple, lemon, pear and yellow grapefruit.

In the red wine category, an Australian shiraz was described as having the flavors of grape, plum, red berry, blueberry, cherry, prune, raisin, banana and vanilla — shiraz is commonly described as being jammy black raspberry-black cherry fruit and spice.

I was astonished by many of the flavor descriptions of both wines. I'd never heard anyone describe a Sauvignon Blanc as possessing raspberry flavor and a shiraz as having the flavor of banana. This made me realize how profoundly my frame of reference for grape varieties and wines impacts my perception of their flavors. Without this frame of reference, the others described a wide range of flavors that fit no particular framework. This confirmed for me that wine comprises both identifiable, tangible building blocks and intangible, subjective flavors. That's why it's best to create a flavor design *after* a solid foundation of tangible building blocks has been established.

Developing a flavor design isn't only a creative process meant to nurture the emotional and spiritual states, it's a celebration of life through wine and food. After all, eating and drinking are emotional and spiritual acts and an expression of living in the moment.

To create a flavor design, match the flavors of the wine with those in the dish. For example, pair the yeasty, bread-like flavor of a quality dry, sparkling wine with the yeasty flavor of freshly baked puff pastry in an appetizer. Enhance the cinnamon spice in a Middle Eastern or North African dish with the apple-like quality in the flavors of Chardonnay. The deep, earthy flavor of a red Burgundy works with the mushroom and earthy flavors of aged French brie.

Pairing the flavors of wine and food is exciting, adventurous, extraordinary and endless!

THE HARMONY CHARTS

Each chapter in Part 2 includes a Harmony Chart highlighting one particular varietal wine (a wine produced primarily from one grape variety). For example, in the chapter on crisp, dry white wines, I've included a chart for Sauvignon Blanc. This chart depicts one creative expression or interpretation of how this specific wine harmonizes with a wide range of herbs, spices, vegetables, fruits, grains and flesh.

The charts follow the principle of concordance (state of agreement or harmony), that the strength and intensity of a particular wine matches the strength and intensity of a specific ingredient. Cumin, for example, has such a strong and intense flavor that it equals the strength and intensity of flavor in icewine. Or, the strength and intense flavor of dark soy sauce equals that of Cabernet Sauvignon.

Remember, this is only one perspective — that of a non-taster and her individual tongue map — and doesn't include all the countless ingredients you may feel work well with specific wines. Designing a flavor partnership is one's creative expression. Use the charts as a foundation from which to create your own.

THE ART OF WINE TASTING

The best way to get the most out of a glass of wine is to embrace the art of tasting it, fully experiencing the tastes and flavors. Tasting wine includes the use of your sight, smell and, of course, taste.

AN EYE FOR BEAUTY

Appearance tells us a great deal about the wine. Look for clarity and color. Wines should be bright and clean, free of floating particles or sediment.

A wine's color is determined by the interaction of many elements. The grape variety, the geography and climate of the region and vineyard in which the grapes are grown, the time of year in which the grapes are picked, the thickness of the grapes' skins and the way the juice is vinified all contribute to a wine's color. As wine ages in the bottle in the wine cellar, its color continues to transform.

To view a wine's color, hold the glass's stem or base and place the glass in front of a white background, such as a tablecloth. The color, whether white or red, can vary tremendously. White wines range from pale green to yellow to golden, depending on their sugar content and oak and cellar aging. As white wines age, they gain color (although most whites are produced to be consumed immediately). Unlike whites, reds degrade in color with age, from deep purple when young to brownish brick and faded at the rim when older.

STOP TO SMELL THE ROSES

We have the ability to identify more than 10,000 odors with our nose. As a result, smelling wine can be frustrating for some, exciting for others. Recognizing a particular aroma in wine is one thing. Finding the word to describe the smell is another. But this is where the fun begins for wine lovers.

The art of smelling wine starts with swirling the glass. This adds oxygen to the wine, releasing the aroma that rises to the surface of the glass. To experience the aroma or bouquet, put your nose into the glass, allowing the rim to touch your forehead. *Gently* sniff. There's a patch of yellow tissue in the nose called the olfactory epithelium, or what I refer to as the wine writer's tool. Located at the top of the nose cavity, this tissue detects odors. If you sniff too aggressively, the alcohol in the wine can numb this tissue, leaving you incapable of smelling anything else for a while. So sniff gently.

Is the aroma pleasant or unpleasant? Is the scent mild, moderate or assertive? The next step is to identify and describe what you smell. The challenge is to find specific words to articulate your experience.

WINE AROMA WHEEL

Wine is like literature, music and art —
we're all entitled to our individual experiences. Ann Noble, a professor emerita of
enology at University of California, Davis,
created the Wine Aroma Wheel with this
individuality in mind. She says that the goal
of the wheel is to encourage the use of a language that describes wine in a way that can
be understood by many, not a dogmatically
determined language understood by only a
few. In short, language that's non-judgmental.

"Perception of aroma is not so precise that,
what one person perceives in wine is peach

and another perceives as pear, we have to
force them to use either one or the other
term," says Noble. "Both, in wine aroma, are
close and possibly indistinguishable, but easily
defined with a physical standard." That physical standard is an accessible vocabulary of
concrete words. Terms such as "luscious" or
"harmonious" are subjective, conveying only
one person's liking or disliking. On the other
hand, "rose petals"or "lemon" very specifically describe a wine's aroma or bouquet, and
in a way that is commonly understood.

As a result, the Wine Aroma Wheel has
become an important tool not only for wine

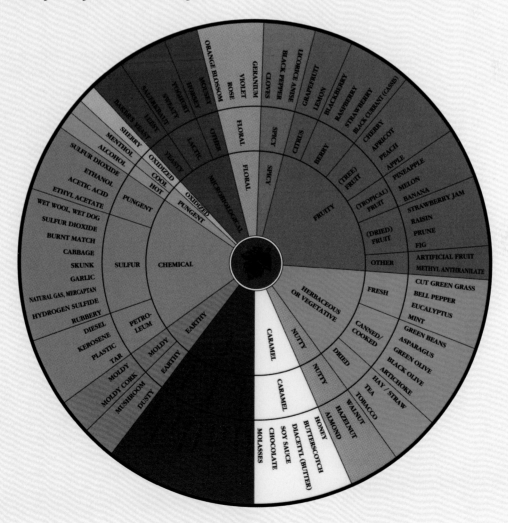

authorities, but for all of us who love to pair wine with food. Made of colored plastic and divided into categories, it helps wine lovers describe the aromas they sense from the nose and palate of a wine. The inner circle provides general terms to describe a wine, such as fruity, nutty or woody. The middle circle includes more specific terms, such as citrus, berry or tropical fruit. The outer circle names specific fruits, such as pineapple, banana or melon. The more you use your imagination and be creative and specific in the description of the aromas or bouquet, the more fun you'll have in choosing wines for your recipes.

PUT YOUR MEMORY WHERE YOUR MOUTH IS

Just as a wine's aroma and bouquet can conjure memories, so too can its tastes and flavors. For me, the candy apple flavor of a refreshing off-dry rosé on a summer day immediately brings back cherished childhood memories of candy apples, the Canadian National Exhibition and hot July afternoons.

Like food, wine has tastes and flavors that work together to create its overall character. To savor this character, take a tiny sip and swish the wine around in your mouth. Make sure it hits every crevice. This is called chewing the wine. Chewing allows your tongue and mouth to perceive the wine's tastes and flavors.

You'll experience the wine's sensations in various parts of your mouth, depending on your individual tongue map. You may detect the wine's sourness first, followed by a bitter aftertaste, or the other way around. The intensity of the sensations is determined by the type of taster you are. If you're a non-

taster, you might revere intense sourness. If you're a super-taster, you'd likely find this sourness too aggressive.

The next step is to aerate the wine while it's in your mouth. Lower your chin, allowing the wine to fall to the inside of your lips. Whistle in backward, pulling air into your mouth to mix with the wine. Adding air to the wine releases the aroma or bouquet in your mouth. This allows you to smell the wine while tasting it. A wine's aroma or bouquet are experienced as flavors in your mouth by way of the retro-nasal pathway.

When chewing and aerating wine, you experience and notice the prominence of certain tastes and flavors. Crisp, dry white wines offer plenty of sourness and fruitiness, while austere reds are fatty and bitter. Use your imagination to find words to specifically describe the characteristics you experience. If the wine tastes like citrus fruit, what specific variety do you taste? Is it yellow or pink grapefruit you experience?

Finally, swallow the wine, paying attention to the length of time the taste and flavors remain in your mouth. Quality wine is like quality coffee — the longer the aftertaste, the better the quality of the wine. "Finishing short" is used by wine lovers to describe a wine that quickly disappears from the palate with little to no aftertaste. "Long finish" describes a wine that has a lingering aftertaste.

PERFECT BALANCE

After looking at, smelling and tasting the wine and assessing its finish, consider its overall balance and quality. Is the aroma or bouquet muted or pronounced? Does the aroma or bouquet communicate the flavors that you are sure to experience on the palate? A great wine is one with a pronounced aroma or bouquet, a well-balanced palate with loads of flavor and a long, pleasant finish. An adequate wine may start off with forward aromas and then slide into muted tastes and flavors on the palate, ending with a short, abrupt finish.

While balance is a sign of quality in wine, every style of wine possesses distinct characteristics for which it's revered. This is the result of the wine's predominant building blocks or their combination. For example, crisp, dry white wines possess tart acidity, more pronounced than what you might find in a big, fat white wine. But this characteristic tart acidity is still balanced with the other elements in the wine, such as its fruitiness.

TRANSITIONING FROM ONE WINE STYLE TO ANOTHER

In the introduction, I pointed to the general pairing rules often recited without any explanation as to their relevance in our wine and food experience. One of these guidelines states we should serve whites before reds. Why? Here's one possible answer.

When entertaining, people often serve a few different wines or wine styles throughout the evening. It's important to remind guests to prepare their palate for the transition. In essence, you're transitioning from one predominant building block to another. Without an understanding of building blocks, your guests might think you're serving inferior wine.

For instance, the sudden change from the sourness of a Sauvignon Blanc to a deliciously creamy and buttery Chardonnay can make the latter taste offensive. More offensive is starting off with the wonderful bitterness of an austere red wine, followed by the sourness of a crisp, dry white. The transition from heavy bitterness to tart and sour is enough to turn people off wine altogether — well, some of us!

It makes sense to serve a wine with sourness before assaulting the palate with something as dominant as bitterness. Acidity refreshes and cleans the palate, opening the way for other taste sensations. Bitterness, however, leaves a lingering taste that may interfere with other flavors.

DETERMINING WINE VALUE

When buying wine for everyday consumption, use its finish to determine if you're getting value. Generally speaking, everyday wines that, after swallowing, last on the palate 1 to 5 seconds are under $10 per bottle. Wines that last on the palate 5 to 10 seconds are generally $10 to $20 per bottle. Wines that linger for more than 10 seconds are considered wines of great quality. At this point, a wine can vary in price. One that remains on the palate for 10 to 20 seconds and is under $20 per bottle offers good value. Wines that finish short yet are pricey may not be worth the investment. If you determine that a particular wine has good length and a reasonable price tag, you may want to stock up on a case or two for everyday consumption.

Regardless of the order of the wines you wish to serve, you and your guests should prepare your palate by taking a small sip of the new wine. Aggressively swish the wine around in your mouth. This isn't meant to be an enjoyable sip, but one to alter the combination of sensations on your palate.

Adding this simple technique to your evening affairs will ensure your guests are satisfied with and confident about your wine style choices and can fully appreciate the harmony between the wines and dishes you matched.

OTHER ELEMENTS AFFECTING PERCEPTION OF FLAVORS IN WINE

There's more to experience than meets the eye, the nose and the palate.

MOOD

Your mood — good or bad, happy or sad — will alter your experience and most certainly affect your perception of wine. Special occasions can make any wine taste fabulous, but stress can cause you to ineffectively assess a wine's character. When you're under stress, your gastrointestinal system becomes acidic, which can cause your palate to be acidic. This acidity can leave an offensive, metallic taste in the mouth. (Kind of like licking a brass lollipop!)

CLIMATE

The time of year and the weather can also influence your decisions with respect to wine with food. For example, you might enjoy pairing a chilled, crisp Sauvignon Blanc with chèvre and fresh greens on a hot summer day. This wine would be less than delicious after spending a long day on the slopes skiing. Instead, you might enjoy a glass of Cabernet Sauvignon while lounging by the fireplace to warm your chilly bones.

TEMPERATURE

Body temperature directly affects how you experience a specific wine and food combination. After spending an afternoon in the sun, you'd likely find a crisp Sauvignon Blanc thirst-quenching and the perfect complement to a light salad with balsamic vinaigrette. After a day of ice fishing or snow skiing, however, this same combination would be less desirable or enjoyable.

As well, the coldness of both wine and food affect flavor. Cold dishes are often more highly spiced to enhance flavor, so choose your wine accordingly. In wine, too cold a temperature will mute a good wine's flavor. On the other hand, wine that is overly warm may seem high in alcohol.

ENVIRONMENT

Environment can taint or enhance your experience of both wine and food. For example, if you're sitting in a crowded, claustrophobic restaurant, you're less likely to linger over or truly savor that big, rich, plummy Cabernet Sauvignon.

EMPLOYING THE BUILDING BLOCKS

The Building Block Principles are an easy system you can use not only to find successful wine and food combinations but also to rework your favorite recipes for pairing success. It's as easy as breaking the recipe down into its building blocks.

READING RECIPES

No doubt you already possess a bookshelf packed with cookbooks. Create your favorite dishes again, this time pairing them with wine styles. There's a simple approach to ensuring recipes will pair well with specific wine styles. Name the building block each ingredient expresses. For example, butter is fatty, salt is salty, yogurt is sour and radicchio is bitter.

After giving each ingredient a building block name, count each group of building blocks. The building block that appears the most determines the style of wine best suited for the recipe. If the recipe possesses three sour ingredients, one salty and one bitter, pair the dish to a sour wine — a crisp, dry white. If the dish has mostly fatty ingredients, such as cream, butter and cheese, match the recipe to a big, fat wine. It's that easy. Here's an example, using a recipe from this cookbook:

Piggyback Oysters

½ lb	250 g	bacon (fatty)
2	2	cans (3 ½ oz/100 g each) smoked oysters (fatty)
1	1	pkg (8 oz/250 g) cream cheese (fatty)

This is obviously a perfect complement to a big, fat white wine.

REWORKING RECIPES

Don't be too shy to take any of the recipes in this cookbook and rework the ingredients so the dish works with a wine of your choosing. Substituting, adding or taking away ingredients can create a new solid foundation of harmony between the wine and the dish.

For example, to ensure a port-style wine harmonized with the Dark Chocolate and Walnut Torte (page 178), I had to rework the recipe twice. The original recipe proved far too sweet, sweeter than the wine, making the port taste tart. In my second attempt, I used 1 Tbsp (15 mL) brown sugar rather than 3 (45 mL) and substituted a regular pie crust for the sweet graham cracker shell. And rather than using 2 cups (500 mL) sweetened condensed milk, as suggested, I substituted 1 cup (250 mL) with unsweetened clotted cream.

The recipe was still too sweet.

In my third attempt, I used 2 cups (500 mL) clotted cream and left out the sweetened condensed milk altogether. I also substituted the semi-sweet cooking chocolate with Belgian bittersweet chocolate, which is higher in cocoa and less sweet. Finally, the recipe was fabulous on its own and paired wonderfully with the port-style wine.

The keys to creating harmony on the palate are creating a solid foundation in your wine and food partnership using the Building Block Principles, then adding your own creative expression when it comes to the flavor design. But, like all principles, these are meant to be challenged. Mary Evely, a respected chef instructor and wine and food affinity consultant in California, is always looking for ways to effectively offset wine and food combinations that theoretically should not work. "Contrast is a fascinating area for continued testing," says Evely. "All the adventurous cooks and diners are encouraged to try some experiments in this field. It's a thrill when you make a successful discovery of your own."

I hope you enjoy experimenting with the recipes as much as I enjoyed inventing, reworking and testing them. As Evely points out, it's always a thrill when you make a successful discovery of your own. Bon appétit!

MATCHING SIMPLE RECIPES TO EVERYDAY WINE STYLES

PART 2

SPARKLING

PREDOMINANT BUILDING BLOCKS

- *Sourness and fruitiness in dry sparkling wines*
- *Sourness, fruitiness and some sweetness in off-dry sparkling wines*

FLAVORS

- *Lemon, peach and tropical to complex, yeasty, toasty and woody*

Sparkling wines that have initially undergone barrel fermentation and aging tend to display creamy texture with vanilla, toasty, yeasty and spicy flavors.

Three main grape varieties produce champagne and quality sparkling wine. Pinot Noir gives backbone and structure. Pinot Meunier provides freshness and aroma, and Chardonnay adds finesse and elegance.

Blanc de noir is a style of white champagne made from Pinot Noir and Pinot Meunier grapes. Blanc de blanc is mostly from Chardonnay. Rosé has a tiny amount of red wine blended into its cuvée (blend).

Twelve communities in Champagne, France, produce Grand Cru (100% quality) Champagne. Forty-one produce Premier Cru (90 to 99% quality). The remaining communities are rated 77 to 89% in quality.

Champagne and quality sparkling wines are made in the classic French *méthode champenoise,* which provides complexity, character and tiny, long-lasting bubbles. Inexpensive bubblies are produced through the transfer, charmat or carbonation method and produce bubblies with less character and shorter-lived bubbles.

When purchasing champagne or sparkling wines, pay attention to their level of sweetness — they range from brut sauvage (bone dry) to doux (sweet). Brut, extra-sec and sec versions work well with breakfast and brunch dishes, appetizers and entrées. Demi-sec and doux bubblies pair well with fruits and desserts.

The regions in the sidebar are stylistically noted for producing sparkling wines.

REGIONS

CHAMPAGNE
France (Champagne)

OTHERS
Australia
Austria
Canada
   (British Columbia, Ontario)
France
Germany
Italy
New Zealand
Spain
United States
   (California, Oregon,
   Washington State)

HARMONY CHART

Brut or Extra-Sec Sparkling Wine

FOOD AFFINITIES

SEAFOOD	MEAT POULTRY	HERBS SPICES	SAUCES	CHEESE NUTS	VEGETABLES FRUITS PASTAS GRAINS
Anchovies	Chicken	Amchur	Chinese light soy sauce	Chèvre	Artichokes
Clams (raw)	Prosciutto	Black cumin	Citrus	Feta	Asparagus
Crab		Black pepper	Sour cream	Parmesan	Bell peppers (raw)
Fish (smoked)		Capers	Vinaigrette	Quark	Cucumbers
Oysters (raw)		Chives	Yogurt		Eggplant
Scallops		Cilantro			Fiddleheads
Shrimp		Coriander			Green beans
Trout		Cumin			Kalamata olives
Tuna		Garlic			Lemons
		Grains of paradise			Lettuces
		Green cardamom			Limes
		Kaffir lime leaves			Snow peas
		Lemon grass			Tomatoes (fresh)
		Oregano			Zucchini
		Tarragon			
		Thyme			

FOOD CHALLENGES

SEAFOOD	MEAT POULTRY	HERBS SPICES	SAUCES	CHEESE NUTS	VEGETABLES FRUITS PASTAS GRAINS
Lobster	Bacon	Cinnamon	Butter	Blue	Avocado
Sturgeon	Foie gras	Cloves	Cream	Brie	Potatoes (mashed)
	Red meats	Curry	Soy	Swiss	Pumpkin
	Sausage	Ginger		Walnuts	Sweet potatoes

BEST METHODS OF PREPARATION
Grilling; smoking; sautéing in oil; uncooked foods, such as salads, crudités and raw fish

COMPLEMENTARY CUISINES
Californian, Mediterranean, vegetarian

BEST SEASONS
Spring, summer

IDEAL OCCASIONS
Barbecue, corn roast or evening grilling, lobster fest, lunch, picnic

Caviar on Potato Crisps

SERVES 4

Potatoes, onion and sour cream are a classic combination. The caviar makes this appetizer extravagant. The sour cream's tangy flavor and creamy texture contrast well with the caviar's crunchy texture and salty flavor.

3	**3**	large white potatoes, peeled
12	**12**	scallions
1 ¼ cups	**300 mL**	vegetable oil
		salt to taste
½ cup	**125 mL**	sour cream
½ cup	**125 mL**	caviar

Slice potatoes into 12 slices, each ¹/₈ inch (0.3 cm) thick. Rinse under cold water and pat dry. Cut the green part of each scallion into 2-inch (5-cm) pieces. Dice the whites. Set aside. In the center of each potato slice, make two ¹/₂-inch (1.25-cm) cuts, ¹/₂ inch (1.25 cm) apart. Weave a scallion green into each potato slice.

In a skillet over moderately high heat, heat oil to almost smoking. Deep-fry potato slices for 2 to 3 minutes, until cooked and golden brown. Drain on paper towel. Salt lightly. Set chips on plates and spoon a dollop of sour cream onto each and top with a dollop of caviar. Sprinkle with diced scallions.

BUILDING BLOCKS

The predominant building blocks are saltiness from the caviar and sourness in the sour cream. A brut or extra-sec sparkling wine with sourness offsets the salty taste and works with the sourness in sour cream.

FLAVORS

Choose a brut or extra-sec sparkling wine with lemon flavor to work with the fishy flavor of caviar and tangy flavor of sour cream.

BUILDING BLOCKS

The predominant building blocks are saltiness from the caviar and sourness in the cream cheese. A brut or extra-sec sparkling wine with sourness offsets the salty taste and works with the sour cream.

FLAVORS

Choose a brut or extra-sec sparkling wine with lemon flavor to work with the fishy flavor of caviar.

Caviar and Cream Cheese

SERVES 4

George and Anna Anagnostou, owners of the Original Greek in Peterborough, Ontario, introduced me to this recipe.

1 cup	250 mL	cream cheese
½ cup	125 mL	caviar
		variety of crackers

Place the cream cheese and caviar in separate serving bowls. Serve cold with crackers.

BUILDING BLOCKS

The predominant building block is sourness from the chèvre. A brut or extra-sec sparkling wine has sourness to work with the chèvre.

FLAVORS

Choose a brut or extra-sec sparkling wine with lemon flavor to work with the tangy flavor of chèvre.

Marinated Chèvre with Sun-Dried Tomatoes and Roasted Garlic

SERVES 4

This is a great cheese dip to serve as an appetizer. I once used the dip left over from a dinner party as the base ingredient for a chicken pizza the next day.

5	5	sun-dried tomatoes
1	1	bulb garlic, skin on
½ cup	125 mL	fresh chèvre
1 Tbsp	15 mL	finely chopped fresh thyme
¼ cup	50 mL	olive oil

Place sun-dried tomatoes in a small bowl and cover with boiling water. Let stand until softened, about 15 minutes. Drain and dice. Place garlic head in a small pan and roast in toaster oven until blackened and tender when pierced with a small, sharp knife, about 20 minutes. Cool slightly. Peel cloves and mash. Set aside.

In a small bowl, fold together the sun-dried tomatoes, garlic, chèvre and thyme. Drizzle with olive oil. Cover with plastic wrap and refrigerate, ideally overnight. Serve with toast or fresh bread.

Chinese Rice-Studded Meatballs with Lime Dipping Sauce

SERVES 4

These rice-coated meatballs are known as *zhen zhu* or "pearls" in Chinese. Steaming the meatballs on bok choy leaves helps to keep them from sticking to the steamer. While this dish can be served as an appetizer, my husband likes it as an entrée.

1 cup	250 mL	jasmine rice
2 to 4	2 to 4	outer bok choy leaves
4	4	scallions
1	1	egg
1/2 cup	125 mL	diced water chestnuts
1 Tbsp	15 mL	each cornstarch, rice vinegar and sesame oil
1 tsp	5 mL	sugar
1/2 tsp	2 mL	chili paste (or as desired)
1 lb	500 g	ground chicken
		salt and pepper to taste
		bok choy leaves (for garnish)
		Lime Dipping Sauce (see page 99)

Place rice in a bowl. Cover with hot water and soak until needed. Set a skillet filled with water on the stove and place a bamboo or metal steamer on the skillet. Line the steamer with bok choy leaves.

In a food processor or blender, add scallions, egg, water chestnuts, cornstarch, rice vinegar, sesame oil, sugar and chili paste. Purée, then transfer mixture to a bowl. Add ground chicken and season with salt and pepper. Mix well. Roll mixture into balls. Drain rice and transfer to a shallow dish. Coat meatballs with damp rice.

Bring the water in the skillet to a boil. Place batches of meatballs in steamer and steam until chicken is cooked through, about 25 minutes. Insert a toothpick in each meatball and place on a platter lined with bok choy leaves. Serve with dipping sauce.

BUILDING BLOCKS

The predominant building block is hot and spicy flavor from the dipping sauce, so the recipe requires a demi-sec sparkling wine with sweetness to offset the heat and spice.

FLAVORS

Choose a demi-sec sparkling wine with lemon-lime flavors to work with the lime flavor in the dipping sauce.

Smoked Salmon Parcels

SERVES 4

This appetizer is always a hit with my guests.

1	1	egg
1 cup	250 mL	low-fat cream cheese, softened
1 cup	250 mL	shredded smoked salmon
2 Tbsp	25 mL	finely chopped fresh dill
1 tsp	5 mL	Worcestershire sauce
		salt and pepper to taste
1	1	sheet frozen puff pastry

Preheat oven to 350°F (180°C). Spray baking sheet with non-stick cooking spray.

In a small bowl, combine egg and cream cheese. Whip with fork until smooth. Fold in salmon, dill and Worcestershire sauce. Season with salt and pepper. Set aside.

Cut the pastry sheet into 2 x 2 inch (5 x 5 cm) squares. Place 1 Tbsp (15 mL) salmon mixture in the center of each square. Fold edges of square over the mixture. Place parcels on baking sheet. Bake 20 to 25 minutes, until pastry is puffed and golden. Serve hot.

Aged Parmesan Frico with Roasted Elephant Garlic and Thyme

SERVES 4

Frico is basically cooked cheese. The disks can be topped with ingredients, as in this recipe. Or, while still hot and flexible, drape the disk over the bottom of a glass to form a basket. It's a nifty container for holding antipasto or other ingredients.

2	2	cloves elephant garlic, skin on
2 Tbsp	25 mL	finely chopped fresh thyme
		black pepper to taste
2 cups	500 mL	grated aged Parmesan
		sour cream (for garnish)

In toaster oven or on the grill, roast garlic cloves. When skin is blackened and garlic is soft, peel and place in a bowl. Mash the cloves and fold in thyme. Season with pepper. Set aside.

Spray a non-stick skillet with non-stick cooking spray and heat over medium heat. Drop 2 Tbsp (25 mL) Parmesan on the skillet and form into a circle. Repeat to make a second circle. Cook on first side for about 2 minutes, until cheese melts, forms a circle and edges are golden. Turn wafers and cook another minute. If cheese disks curl, flatten with a spatula.

Remove from pan and set on paper towel. Repeat until all cheese is used. Spread garlic mixture on each and garnish with a dollop of sour cream. Set on plates and serve immediately.

Greek Yogurt Chicken

SERVES 4

Due to its acidity, yogurt tenderizes meat during roasting or baking and as a marinade. It also keeps flesh moist during cooking. If roasting or baking with yogurt, don't use foil. The acid reacts negatively to the aluminum, changing the yogurt's flavor.

2	2	cloves garlic, minced
1 cup	250 mL	plain yogurt
2 Tbsp	25 mL	each finely chopped fresh oregano, finely chopped fresh parsley and fresh lemon juice
1 tsp	5 mL	lemon zest
pinch	pinch	each salt and pepper
4	4	boneless, skinless chicken breasts

In a bowl, combine garlic, yogurt, oregano, parsley, lemon juice, lemon zest, salt and pepper. Place chicken breasts in a glass baking dish. Add ¼ cup (50 mL) yogurt sauce and coat chicken. Cover and refrigerate overnight. Cover and refrigerate remaining yogurt sauce.

Preheat oven to 375°F (190°C). Bake chicken, uncovered, for 30 minutes, then broil for 5 minutes, until chicken is golden. Spoon reserved chilled yogurt sauce over chicken and serve immediately.

BUILDING BLOCKS

The predominant building block is sourness from the yogurt and lemon juice. A brut or extra-sec sparkling wine with sourness works with these ingredients.

FLAVORS

Choose a brut or extra-sec sparkling wine with lemon flavor to match the tangy flavor of yogurt and lemon flavor of fresh lemon.

The predominant building blocks are saltiness from the prosciutto and cheese and sweetness from the melon. A demi-sec sparkling wine has sourness to offset the saltiness and some sweetness to work with the melon.

FLAVORS

Choose a demi-sec sparkling wine with peach and melon flavors to work with the melon and cantaloupe.

Rolled Prosciutto and Melon with Burrini

SERVES 4

Burrini is an interesting Italian cheese available in most cheese shops or Italian supermarkets. This mild cheese has a pale yellow or ivory rind with a ball of butter tucked inside. The original recipe was created by Ronald Sainte-Pierre. This is my rendition.

2 tsp	10 mL	olive oil
1/2	1/2	sweet red pepper, diced
1/2 cup	125 mL	diced mushrooms
		salt and pepper to taste
1 tsp	5 mL	fresh lemon juice
1/2 lb	250 g	burrini cheese*
1/2 cup	125 mL	diced honeydew melon
1/2 cup	125 mL	diced cantaloupe
1 tsp	5 mL	finely chopped fresh oregano
1 tsp	5 mL	finely chopped fresh chives
4	4	6-inch (15-cm) slices prosciutto

*Burrini can be substituted with any white, soft ripened cheese and 1/2 cup (125 mL) creamed butter.

In a small skillet over medium heat, heat oil. Sauté red pepper and mushrooms until pepper is soft. Add a little water if needed. Season with salt and pepper. Sprinkle lemon juice over the mixture. Remove mixture from skillet and set aside to cool.

Slice cheese in half and remove the butter ball. In a large bowl, whip butter until doubled in volume. Dice cheese and add to butter. Stir in melon, cantaloupe, oregano and chives. Add red pepper and mushroom mixture and mix well.

On a sheet of waxed paper, lay out each prosciutto slice. Spread the filling evenly over prosciutto until about 1/4 inch (0.5 cm) thick, leaving space at the edges. Carefully roll prosciutto lengthwise into a cylinder. Place rolls on a cookie tray, seam side down and refrigerate for 1 hour, until butter is firm. With a warm, dry knife, cut rolled prosciutto into 1/2-inch (1.25-cm) slices.

Fried Calamari with Tzatziki

SERVES 4

Chef Anna Anagnostou created this recipe, which I order whenever dining at the Original Greek in Peterborough, Ontario. Anna was gracious enough to share her recipe with me so that I could make it at home — and now I share it with you.

TZATZIKI

2 cups	500 mL	plain yogurt
3	3	cloves garlic, minced
½	½	cucumber, finely shredded
1 Tbsp	15 mL	finely chopped fresh dill
1 tsp	5 mL	olive oil
pinch	pinch	salt

CALAMARI

12	12	medium squid
1 cup	250 mL	flour (for dredging)
1 Tbsp	15 mL	garlic powder
½ tsp	2 mL	each paprika, salt and white pepper
1	1	egg, beaten
		vegetable oil (for deep-frying)
2 Tbsp	25 mL	fresh lemon juice
4	4	fresh lemon wedges (for garnish)

To make tzatziki, place yogurt in cheesecloth or a coffee filter. Put bowl underneath. Refrigerate overnight to strain out excess liquid. In a bowl, combine yogurt, garlic, cucumber, dill, oil and salt. Blend well. Cover and refrigerate until needed.

To make calamari, cut squid into rings, about 1 inch (2.5 cm) thick. Wash and let dry. In a small bowl, combine flour, garlic powder, paprika, salt and pepper. In another small bowl, add egg. Dip squid in egg wash. Dredge in flour mixture, then shake off excess flour. In a large pan over high heat, heat oil until almost smoking. Place squid in oil and deep-fry for about 2 minutes, until squid is firm but not rubbery. Drizzle with lemon juice and serve hot with tzatziki and lemon wedges.

BUILDING BLOCKS

The predominant building block is sourness from the yogurt and lemon juice. A brut or extra sec sparkling wine with sourness works with these ingredients.

FLAVORS

Choose a brut or extra sec sparkling wine with lemon flavor to work with the freshly squeezed lemon juice.

Wild Rice and Bulgar Salad with Lemon, Garlic and Olive Oil

SERVES 4

I created this recipe to accompany barbecued chicken legs, but it's substantial enough to be an entrée. The lemon and raw garlic are fabulous together. As a non-taster, I often use six to eight garlic cloves, but I've altered the amount for this recipe.

6 to 8	6 to 8	large black olives, sliced
2	2	tomatoes, diced
2	2	cloves garlic, minced (or as desired)
1 cup	250 mL	each cooked wild rice and cooked bulgar
1/2 cup	125 mL	each cooked green peas and chopped fresh parsley
1/4 cup	50 mL	olive oil (or as needed)
		chili paste (as desired)
		juice from 1 to 2 lemons (to taste)
		salt and pepper to taste

In a large bowl, combine all ingredients. Toss and serve.

Quiche Kisses

SERVES 4

I've seen this egg dish made by several cooks and with a variety of ingredients. It's a fancy way to serve quiche as an appetizer. However, the kisses are also an inventive way to serve eggs at brunch with wine.

1 Tbsp	15 mL	butter
3	3	mushrooms, diced
2	2	scallions, diced
1/2	1/2	green pepper, diced
1/2 cup	125 mL	diced smoked ham
4	4	eggs, beaten
1/2 cup	125 mL	shredded cheddar
		salt and pepper to taste
6	6	slices fresh bread

Preheat oven to 300°F (150°C). In a skillet, melt butter over medium heat. Add mushrooms, scallions, green pepper and

BUILDING BLOCKS

The predominant building block is sourness from the lemon and tomatoes. A brut or extra-sec sparkling wine with sourness works with these ingredients.

FLAVORS

Choose a brut or extra-sec sparkling wine with lemon flavor to match the lemon flavor.

BUILDING BLOCKS

The predominant building blocks are saltiness from the smoked ham and fattiness from the butter and cheese. A brut or extra-sec sparkling wine with sourness and fattiness offsets the salt and works with the creamy, buttery texture of butter and cheese.

FLAVORS

Choose a brut or extra-sec sparkling wine with complex yeasty and toasty flavors to match the earthy flavor of mushrooms and smoky flavor of ham.

ham. Sauté until tender. Remove from heat and pour into a bowl. Add the eggs, then fold in cheese. Season with salt and pepper.

Spray a muffin tin with non-stick cooking spray. Flatten a slice of bread with your palm. Cup the slice and place in a muffin cup. Press bread against the sides and bottom. Drop a heaping tablespoon of egg mixture into the cup. Repeat for remaining bread.

Bake 10 to 15 minutes, until eggs are set and bread is toasted. Let cool. Wrap and refrigerate until morning or eat immediately.

Swiss Egg Brioche

SERVES 4

"Brioche" is French and refers to yeast bread rich in butter and eggs. Kids love it for breakfast. Egg brioche can be served as an appetizer or a brunch dish accompanied by sparkling wine.

4	4	brioches
2 Tbsp	25 mL	butter, melted
4	4	large eggs
4	4	slices bacon, cooked and diced
½ cup	125 mL	shredded Swiss cheese
2 Tbsp	25 mL	finely chopped fresh chives
		salt and pepper to taste

Preheat oven to 350°F (180°C). Carefully cut about 1 inch (2.5 cm) off the top of each brioche and gently pull out the inside, making a shell. Press your fingers along the walls of each brioche to make a bigger cup. Brush the inside of each cup and the tops with butter.

Spray a six-cup muffin tin with non-stick cooking spray and place the brioches in the cups. Crack an egg into each shell. In a bowl, combine remaining ingredients. Place a dollop of this mixture on each egg. Bake 15 minutes, until eggs are cooked. For the last 5 minutes, arrange the brioche tops, cut sides up, in a shallow baking pan and bake until golden. Place tops on each brioche and serve hot.

EGGS AND WINE

Eggs are traditionally considered a difficult ingredient to pair to wine. They are alkaline, which is believed to clash with wine's acidity. However, most egg dishes contain other ingredients, making it easy to pair egg dishes to wine. Just distinguish the predominant building block in the dish and match this to the predominant building block in the wine.

BUILDING BLOCKS

The predominant building block is fattiness from the pastry, butter, bacon and cheese. A brut or extra-sec sparkling wine that has undergone barrel fermentation and aging has enough fattiness to work with this dish.

FLAVORS

Choose a brut or extra-sec sparkling wine with full body, creamy texture and yeasty, toasty flavors that work with the smoky flavor of bacon.

CRISP, DRY WHITES

PREDOMINANT BUILDING BLOCKS

- *Sourness and fruitiness*

FLAVORS

- *Lemon, lime, gooseberry, grapefruit, green apple and pineapple*
- *Other flavors include floral, grassy and mineral-like*

The factors that determine wines that fall into this style are the grape variety, the geography, climate and soil conditions of the wine region, and the winemaking techniques employed. Certain grape varieties, such as Sauvignon Blanc and Riesling, naturally have a high level of acidity. During fermentation, the juice is fermented in temperature-controlled stainless steel tanks. This style of fermentation allows the grapes to retain their natural malic (green apple-like) acidity and fruitiness.

Crisp, dry white wines are often referred to as food wines because the crisp acidity cleans the palate between bites. They can range in style from delicate with steely acidity and gooseberry fruit to luscious and full with juicy lime and pineapple fruit character. Every winemaker produces crisp, dry white wines with their own distinctive flavor profile.

Wines within this style taste great on hot summer days and pair well with salad vinaigrettes, fresh and grilled vegetables and grilled chicken and seafood.

The regions at right are stylistically noted for producing crisp, dry white wines.

REGIONS

SAUVIGNON BLANC
Canada (British Columbia, Ontario)
Chile (Casablanca Valley)
France (Bordeaux, Languedoc, Loire)
Italy (Friuli)
New Zealand
South Africa
Spain (Penedes, Rueda)
United States (California)

DRY RIESLING
Canada (British Columbia, Ontario)
France (Alsace)
Germany
United States (Oregon, Washington State)

OTHERS
Aligoté – Canada (Ontario)
Chenin Blanc –South Africa, United States (California)
Cortese di Gavi – Italy (Piedmont)
DOC Frascati – Italy (Latium/Lazio)
DOC Vernaccia di San Gimignano – Italy (Florence)
Grüner Veltliner – Austria
Muscadet – France (Loire)
Orvieto - Italy (Umbria)
Verdicchio dei Castelli di Jesi – Italy (The Marches)
Vinho Verde – Portugal (Vinho Verde)
Viognier – France (Côtes du Rhone)
Viura – Spain (Rioja)

HARMONY CHART

Sauvignon Blanc

FOOD AFFINITIES

SEAFOOD	MEAT POULTRY	HERBS SPICES	SAUCES	CHEESE NUTS	VEGETABLES FRUITS PASTAS GRAINS
Anchovies	Chicken (smoked)	Amchur	Chinese light soy sauce	Chèvre	Artichokes
Crab	Prosciutto	Black cumin	Citrus	Feta	Asparagus
Clams (raw)		Black pepper	Sour cream	Parmesan	Bell peppers (raw)
Fish (smoked)		Capers	Vinaigrette	Quark	Cucumbers
Oysters (raw)		Chives	Yogurt		Eggplant
Scallops		Cilantro			Fiddleheads
Shrimp		Coriander			Green beans
Trout		Cumin			Kalamata olives
Tuna		Garlic			Lemons
		Grains of paradise			Lettuces
		Green cardamom			Limes
		Kaffir lime leaves			Snow peas
		Lemon grass			Tomatoes (fresh)
		Oregano			Zucchini
		Tarragon			
		Thyme			

FOOD CHALLENGES

SEAFOOD	MEAT POULTRY	HERBS SPICES	SAUCES	CHEESE NUTS	VEGETABLES FRUITS PASTAS GRAINS
Lobster	Bacon	Cinnamon	Butter	Blue	Avocado
Sturgeon	Foie gras	Cloves	Cream	Brie	Potatoes (mashed)
	Red meats	Curry	Soy	Swiss	Pumpkin
	Sausage	Ginger		Walnuts	Sweet potatoes

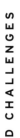

BEST METHODS OF PREPARATION
Grilling; smoking; sautéing in oil; uncooked foods, such as salads, crudités and raw fish

COMPLEMENTARY CUISINES
Californian, Mediterranean, vegetarian

BEST SEASONS
Spring, summer

IDEAL OCCASIONS
Barbecue, corn roast or evening grilling, lobster fest, lunch, picnic

Grilled Asparagus and Prosciutto Wraps

SERVES 4

This recipe seems to be popular among many foodies — a similar version appears in James Beard's cookbook *Hors D'oeuvre and Canapés*.

1	**1**	bunch asparagus, washed and dried
½ lb	**250 g**	prosciutto, sliced

Hold the bottom end of the asparagus stem in one hand and gently bend the stalk with the other. The stalk will break at its most tender point. Wrap each asparagus in a slice of prosciutto. Grill until the prosciutto is crispy. Serve immediately.

BUILDING BLOCKS

The predominant building block is saltiness from the prosciutto. A crisp, dry white has sourness to offset the saltiness.

FLAVORS

Choose a crisp, dry white with grassy and herbal flavors to work with the asparagus.

BUILDING BLOCKS

The predominant building block is the saltiness from capers, smoked salmon and lumpfish roe and sourness from the lemon and sour cream. A crisp, dry white with sourness offsets the saltiness and works with the lemon and sour cream.

FLAVORS

Choose a crisp, dry white with lemon flavor to work with the fish flavor and draw out the lemon flavor.

Onion Parcels of Smoked Salmon and Cream Cheese with Chives

SERVES 4

Chef Momir Filipovic created the original version of this recipe. I've been making this appetizer for over a decade — this is my current rendition.

2	2	large white onions, peeled
5	5	capers, drained
1/4 lb	125 g	smoked salmon, boned and skinned
1/2 cup	125 mL	low-fat cream cheese
2 tsp	10 mL	fresh lemon juice
8	8	chives
1/4 cup	50 mL	sour cream, drained
1/4 cup	50 mL	lumpfish roe

In a pot of boiling salted water, poach onions for 10 minutes, until soft. Drain and set aside until cool. In a food processor or blender, purée capers and smoked salmon. Add cream cheese and lemon juice. Blend well and set aside.

Separate the onion layers and slice lengthwise into strips about 2 1/2 inches (6.5 cm) wide. Keep 20 of the best strips. Fit a piping bag with a plain tip and fill with smoked salmon mixture. (Or fill a small plastic bag and snip a small hole in one corner.) Pipe 1 tsp (5 mL) mixture onto each onion strip. Fold two sides of onion over the mixture. Place parcels on a plate, seam side down. Refrigerate for at least 1 hour.

On four chilled plates, arrange five parcels in the shape of a flower. Use two chives for each stem. Fill a cleaned piping bag with sour cream and pipe 1 tsp (5 mL) into the center of each flower. Sprinkle lumpfish roe on sour cream.

Cold Orzo Salad with Grilled Shrimp, Tomatoes, Baby Arugula and Coriander

SERVES 4

This dish is colorful, healthy and so simple to make. I developed it for a food feature article. Later, when spending an afternoon at a friend's cottage, I learned that another guest had cut out the article from the paper. It seemed to be a hit.

1 cup	250 mL	dried orzo pasta
12	12	medium shrimp, peeled, deveined and cooked
1/4 cup	50 mL	olive oil
		juice from 1/2 lemon (more if desired)
2 Tbsp	25 mL	finely chopped fresh cilantro
1	1	yellow tomato, chopped
1	1	red tomato, chopped
1/2 cup	125 mL	chopped arugula
		salt and pepper to taste

In a large pot of boiling, salted water, cook pasta until al dente, 7 to 10 minutes, stirring occasionally. Drain and rinse under cold water. Set aside. Grill shrimp on barbecue until charred, about 3 minutes per side. Let cool.

In a bowl, mix together olive oil, lemon juice and coriander. Just before serving, pour vinaigrette over pasta and fold in tomatoes and arugula. Season with salt and pepper. Put salad on plates and place three shrimp on each salad. Serve immediately.

The predominant building block is sourness from the rice vinegar and saltiness in the Parmesan. A crisp, dry white with sourness works with the vinegar and offsets the Parmesan.

FLAVORS

Choose a crisp, dry white with grassy or herbal flavors to match the flavors of the vegetables.

WINE VINEGARS AND WINE

Recently, wine vinegars have become popular. In fact, there's now a specialty item called "varietal wine vinegar," produced from a varietal wine made primarily from one specific grape variety.

Many people assume that a varietal wine vinegar should match with that same varietal wine, but this combination doesn't always harmonize. Even though they're produced from the same grape, the vinegar is usually more sour than the wine. This causes the wine to taste metallic and unpleasant. To have the combination harmonize, the wine must be more acidic than the vinegar.

To reduce the sourness of a wine vinegar used in a salad, add more proteins. Try cheese, nuts and flesh, such as chicken or ham.

Salad of Fresh Corn and Bell Peppers

SERVES 4

For summer dining with wine, I'm a big fan of fresh vegetables in salads. I particularly love the crunchy texture of fresh corn cut from the cob. This colorful salad also pleases the eye.

SALAD

2	**2**	ears fresh corn, cooked and cut from cobs
½	**½**	each red and yellow bell peppers, julienned
		arugula leaves (as needed)

VINAIGRETTE

3 Tbsp	**45 mL**	rice wine vinegar (or as needed)
3 Tbsp	**45 mL**	olive oil (or as needed)
3 Tbsp	**45 mL**	freshly grated Parmesan
		cracked black pepper to taste

Combine corn, peppers and arugula. In a small bowl, combine vinaigrette ingredients. Toss vinaigrette into salad. Divide among plates. Top with cheese and season with pepper.

Cold Mediterranean Pasta Salad

SERVES 4

While researching and writing a feature story about cold pasta salads, I fell in love with them. There are so many shapes and textures of pasta and so many sauces to enhance them!

1 lb	**500 g**	fettuccine
2	**2**	ripe plum tomatoes, chopped
1 cup	**250 mL**	crumbled feta cheese
¼ cup	**50 mL**	kalamata olives
3 Tbsp	**45 mL**	finely chopped fresh dill
¼ cup	**50 mL**	olive oil
		juice from ½ lemon (more if desired)
		salt and pepper to taste

In a large pot of boiling, salted water, cook pasta until al dente, 7 to 10 minutes, stirring occasionally. Drain and rinse under cold water. In a large bowl, mix together the pasta, tomatoes, feta, olives and dill. In a small bowl, whisk together oil and lemon juice. Toss dressing into salad. Season with salt and pepper. Serve immediately.

BUILDING BLOCKS

The predominant building blocks are sourness from the tomatoes, feta and lemon. A crisp, dry white with sourness works with these ingredients.

FLAVORS

Choose a crisp, dry white with lemon flavor to match the lemon flavor of the vinaigrette.

Romano and Basil Gateau

SERVES 4

"Gateau" is French for "cake." This gateau freezes well, but if you intend to freeze it, don't drizzle the olive oil over it. Instead, add olive oil just before serving.

1 cup	250 mL	ricotta cheese
1 cup	250 mL	grated Romano cheese
3/4 cup	175 mL	low-fat cream cheese
4	4	eggs
2	2	cloves garlic
1 1/2 cups	375 mL	fresh basil
2 Tbsp	25 mL	melted butter
1 Tbsp	15 mL	flour
		juice of 1 lemon
		salt, pepper, grated nutmeg to taste
3/4 cup	175 mL	sour cream
		sliced tomatoes (for garnish)
		olive oil (as needed)
		pine nuts (for garnish)

In a large bowl, combine ricotta, Romano and cream cheese. In a food processor or blender, add eggs, garlic, basil, butter, flour, lemon juice, salt, pepper and nutmeg. Process, slowly adding cream cheese mixture. Pulsate to blend. Add sour cream and pulse until just mixed.

Preheat oven to 325°F (160°C). Pour mixture into a well-greased 9-inch (2.5-L) springform pan. Bake 50 minutes, until a wooden skewer inserted into the gateau comes out clean. Cool on rack, then remove from pan. To serve, slice with a hot knife and arrange over tomato slices. Drizzle with olive oil and sprinkle with pine nuts.

BUILDING BLOCKS

The predominant building block is sourness from the lemon, sour cream and tomato. A crisp, dry white with more sourness works with these ingredients.

FLAVORS

Choose a crisp, dry white with plenty of lemon flavor to match this gateau's lemon-tangy flavor.

BUILDING BLOCKS

The predominant building block is sourness from the white wine and feta. A matching crisp, dry white with sourness works with the wine and feta.

FLAVORS

Choose a crisp, dry white with lemon flavor to match the tangy flavor of feta.

Shrimp Sauvignon Blanc

SERVES 4

Southbrook Farms Winery in Maple, Ontario, gave me this recipe many years ago. I've since made this dish countless times, even using bread crumbs from low-carbohydrate bread for my friends practicing a low-carb lifestyle.

½ cup	125 mL	Sauvignon Blanc
2	2	cloves garlic, minced
¼ cup	50 mL	olive oil
2 lb	1 kg	fresh shrimp, peeled and deveined
1 cup	250 mL	coarse dry bread crumbs
¾ cup	175 mL	crumbled feta cheese
1 Tbsp	15 mL	finely chopped fresh thyme
		freshly ground pepper to taste

In a glass bowl, combine wine, half the garlic and 2 Tbsp (25 mL) olive oil. Stir in shrimp, cover and refrigerate for 2 hours. In another bowl, combine remaining garlic and olive oil, the bread crumbs, feta, thyme and pepper.

Preheat oven to 450°F (230°C). Drain shrimp and arrange in a heatproof baking dish. Spread bread-crumb topping evenly over the shrimp. Bake, uncovered, 10 to 15 minutes, until bread crumbs are golden. Serve immediately.

Seafood Salad with Feta and Lemon Vinaigrette

SERVES 4

True Greek feta cheese is made from goat's milk and is tangy tasting. North American versions are often made from cow's milk and are milder. The tangy flavor of Greek feta works nicely with crisp, dry white wines.

24	**24**	mussels, scrubbed and debearded
¼ lb	**125 g**	each sea scallops and medium shrimp, peeled and deveined

LEMON AND FETA VINAIGRETTE

⅓ cup	**75 mL**	crumbled feta cheese
1 Tbsp	**15 mL**	finely chopped fresh thyme
2 tsp	**10 mL**	fresh lemon juice
		salt and pepper to taste
¼ cup	**50 mL**	olive oil (or as needed)

1	**1**	head bibb lettuce (as needed)

In a steamer set over boiling water, steam seafood until mussels open, scallops are tender and shrimp are pink, about 4 minutes. Discard unopened mussels. Let seafood cool.

To make the vinaigrette, combine feta, thyme, lemon juice, salt and pepper in a food processor. With motor running, slowly add the olive oil to form a vinaigrette consistency.

Line plates with lettuce leaves. Arrange seafood on leaves and drizzle with vinaigrette. Serve immediately.

BUILDING BLOCKS

The predominant building block is sourness from the feta and lemon. A crisp, dry white with sourness matches the feta and lemon.

FLAVORS

Choose a crisp, dry white with lemon flavor to match the tangy and lemon flavors of feta and lemon.

BUILDING BLOCKS

The predominant building block is sourness from the dry white wine and tomatoes. A crisp, dry white wine with sourness works with the wine and tomatoes.

FLAVORS

Choose a crisp, dry white with herbaceous or grassy flavors to match the flavors of asparagus, tomatoes and fresh herbs.

Asparagus and Tomato Salad with Fresh Herbs

SERVES 4

An old food and wine pairing rule dictates that asparagus doesn't work well with wine. Humbug! This recipe is proof that rules need to be broken. Blanched or steamed, asparagus is highly flavorful and an excellent wine partner when other ingredients are included.

½ cup	125 mL	crisp, dry white wine
¼ cup	50 mL	olive oil
1	1	green onion, finely chopped
1 Tbsp	15 mL	each finely chopped fresh chervil and fresh chives
		salt and pepper to taste
1 lb	500 g	asparagus, trimmed, blanched, cut on diagonal
1 lb	500 g	tomatoes, sliced

In a saucepan over medium heat, reduce wine by half. Blend in oil to create an emulsion. Stir in the onion, fresh herbs, salt and pepper. Remove from heat and pour into a small bowl. Toss asparagus and tomatoes with desired amount of dressing. Serve immediately.

Cold Buckwheat Noodles with Thai Basil Vinaigrette

SERVES 4

If you're a non-taster like me, you'll want to increase the amount of lime juice and fish sauce.

THAI BASIL VINAIGRETTE

¼ cup	50 mL	fresh lime juice
2 Tbsp	25 mL	finely chopped Thai basil (or sweet basil)
2 Tbsp	25 mL	fish sauce
1 tsp	5 mL	sugar
		salt and pepper to taste
		peanut oil (as needed)
¾ lb	375 g	dried buckwheat noodles
		vegetable oil (as needed)
2	2	scallions, chopped
		finely chopped peanuts (as desired)

To make the vinaigrette, in a food processor or blender add all the vinaigrette ingredients except peanut oil. Purée, adding peanut oil in a steady stream until smooth. Pour vinaigrette into bowl. Cover and refrigerate until needed.

Meanwhile, in a pot of boiling, salted water, cook noodles until al dente, 2 to 4 minutes. Drain and rinse under cold water. In a bowl, toss noodles with just enough vegetable oil to coat and to keep from sticking together. Combine vinaigrette with noodles. Add more lime juice and fish sauce if needed. Sprinkle scallions and peanuts on top. Serve immediately.

BUILDING BLOCKS

The predominant building blocks are saltiness from the fish sauce and sourness from the lime juice. A crisp, dry white with sourness offsets the saltiness and works with the lime juice.

FLAVORS

Choose a crisp, dry white with lemon-lime flavor to match the lime and work with the strong fishy taste of fish sauce.

The predominant building blocks are saltiness from the soy sauce and sourness from the rice vinegar. A crisp, dry white with sourness offsets the saltiness in soy sauce and works with the rice vinegar.

FLAVORS

Choose a crisp, dry white with pineapple flavor to match the citrus, pineapple flavor of rice vinegar.

Asian Pasta Salad with Grilled Jumbo Shrimp

SERVES 4

Use the Asian version of sesame oil for this recipe. Made from hulled, toasted sesame seeds, it's amber and has a distinctive, nutty flavor.

8	8	jumbo shrimp, peeled, deveined and cooked
1/4 cup	50 mL	sesame seeds
1/4 cup	50 mL	Chinese light soy sauce
3 Tbsp	45 mL	rice vinegar
2 Tbsp	25 mL	Asian sesame oil
pinch	pinch	salt and pepper
1 lb	500 g	Chinese egg noodles
2	2	medium scallions, trimmed and sliced thin on bias
1/2 cup	125 mL	bean sprouts

Prepare grill until very hot. Grill shrimp until flesh is marked with golden grill lines, about 3 minutes each side. Set aside. In a small, dry skillet, toast the sesame seeds over medium-high heat until lightly browned, about 2 minutes. Let cool. In a bowl, combine soy sauce, vinegar, sesame oil, salt and pepper. Set aside.

Fill a large bowl with boiling water. Add noodles and let soak for about 10 seconds, just until soft. Do not oversoak. Drain and rinse under cold water. Transfer noodles to a large mixing bowl. Toss with dressing. Fold in scallions and sprouts. Sprinkle with sesame seeds. Toss and add more soy sauce if needed. Set salad on plates and put 2 shrimp on top of each. Serve immediately.

Rotini Mediterranean

SERVES 4

An integral ingredient in Mediterranean cuisine, capers possess a sharp piquant and salty taste. Because of these flavors, dishes containing capers are best served with wines high in acidity, such as dry, sparkling or crisp, dry white wines.

2 Tbsp	25 mL	olive oil (or as needed)
2	2	cloves garlic, minced
4	4	boneless, skinless chicken breasts
½ cup	125 mL	white wine
1	1	bunch green onions, chopped
1 cup	250 mL	diced tomatoes
½ cup	125 mL	chopped olives
1 Tbsp	15 mL	capers
1 lb	500 g	rotini
½ cup	125 mL	crumbled feta cheese

In a large skillet, heat oil over medium heat. Add garlic and sauté until aromatic. Add chicken breasts. Sear until golden on each side, about 3 minutes. Add wine. Reduce heat to low and simmer for 3 to 5 minutes, until wine is reduced by half. Add green onions and tomatoes and cook until chicken is white inside, 10 to 15 minutes. Add olives and capers and cook another 5 minutes. Keep hot.

Meanwhile, in a pot of boiling, salted water, cook rotini until al dente, 7 to 10 minutes. Drain. Remove chicken from pan. Pour olive mixture over rotini. Toss. Divide among plates. Slice chicken breasts and lay on rotini. Sprinkle breasts and pasta with feta and serve immediately.

BUILDING BLOCKS

The predominant building blocks are saltiness from the capers and sourness from the tomatoes and feta. A crisp, dry white offsets the saltiness and works with the sourness in the tomatoes and feta.

FLAVORS

Choose a crisp, dry white with tangy lemon flavor to match the tangy flavors from the wine and feta.

BUILDING BLOCKS

The predominant building block is sourness from the tomato salsa and lime juice. A crisp, dry white wine with sourness works with the salsa and lime juice.

FLAVORS

Choose a crisp, dry white with grassy flavor to bring out the subtle flavors of cumin and cilantro.

Tex-Mex Turkey Burgers with Corn Salsa

SERVES 4

The tortilla chip filling adds a different texture to these burgers. You can use ground chicken instead of turkey.

TURKEY BURGERS

1 ½ lb	675 g	ground turkey
½ cup	125 mL	each tortilla chips, crushed, and mild tomato salsa (of choice)
½ tsp	2 mL	each ground cumin and salt
¼ tsp	1 mL	pepper

CORN SALSA

1 cup	250 mL	mild tomato salsa (of choice)
½ cup	125 mL	corn (fresh or frozen)
2 Tbsp	25 mL	chopped fresh cilantro
1 Tbsp	15 mL	fresh lime juice
4	4	flour tortillas

In a large bowl, combine burger ingredients. Form meat into four large patties. Over medium heat, broil or grill burgers 10 to 12 minutes, turning once, until no longer pink inside. Keep warm until ready to serve. In a small bowl, combine salsa ingredients. Set aside.

Spray a large non-stick pan with non-stick cooking spray and place over medium heat. Warm tortillas in pan, about 30 seconds per side. Place patties on tortillas and top with corn salsa. Serve immediately.

Fresh Tomato Pasta

SERVES 4

This is an ideal dish to make when fresh tomatoes are in season. If you're a super-taster with a sensitive palate, cut back on the garlic and red chili peppers.

1 lb	500 g	spaghetti
1 Tbsp	15 mL	olive oil
5	5	cloves garlic, minced
2 cups	500 mL	diced fresh tomatoes
2	2	small red chili peppers, finely diced (for more heat, leave seeds in)
		salt and pepper to taste

In a large pot of boiling, salted water, cook spaghetti until al dente, 7 to 10 minutes. Drain. Meanwhile, in a saucepan, heat oil over medium heat and sauté garlic until aromatic, about 2 minutes. Add tomatoes and chilies. Heat through, about 3 minutes. Don't overcook. Season with salt and pepper. Place the pasta on plates and add sauce.

PAIRING PASTA AND SAUCES WITH WINE

When marrying wine with pasta and sauces, consider the noodle's shape and consistency and the sauce's weight, texture and flavor. Marry the weight of the sauce to the density of the noodle to the weight of the wine. Otherwise, one element will dominate the others, causing the combination to be imbalanced in flavor and texture. Here are some examples to get you going.

BUILDING BLOCKS

The predominant building block is sourness from the tomatoes. A crisp, dry white wine with sourness works with the tomatoes.

FLAVORS

Choose a crisp, dry white with herbal flavor to work with the fresh tomato and heavy garlic flavor.

NOODLE	SAUCE	WINE STYLE
Thin, delicate (angel hair, spaghettini)	Light (broth)	Crisp, dry white; dry rosé; light, fruity red
Thick (fettuccine)	Heavy (cream, meat)	Big, fat white (cream); austere red (meat)
With holes or ridges (mostaccioli or radiatore)	Chunky (seafood, meat)	Well-balanced, medium-bodied, smooth white; big, fat white (seafood); red with forward fruit; austere red (meat)
Twisted (rotini)	Chunky or heavy (vegetable, cheese, meat)	Crisp, dry white (vegetable); big fat white (cheese); austere red (meat)
Tube (manicotti)	Heavy (cream, cheese, meat)	Big, fat white (cream); austere red (meat)

WELL-BALANCED, MEDIUM-BODIED, **SMOOTH** WHITES

PREDOMINANT BUILDING BLOCKS

- *Balance of sourness and fruitiness with some fattiness*

FLAVORS

- *Light and peachy to lush and tropical*
- *Other flavors include nutty, mineral-like and floral*

Grape variety, geography, the wine region's climate and soil, and winemaking techniques determine the wines that fall into this style. Many wine regions around the world produce well-balanced, medium-bodied, smooth white wines. They're often produced in cool regions, such as Canada, Oregon, Burgundy or Northern Italy. However, they can also come from the cooler regions of warmer countries, such as Chile. Chardonnay is a classic example of a wine produced in this style.

Different techniques help to balance these medium-bodied white wines in their predominant building blocks. Grapes in cooler climates ripen slowly and retain some of their natural acidity. Through a process called malolactic fermentation, the winemaker may transform some of this malic acid (apple-like) to lactic acid (creamier, milk-like). The wines might also be aged for a short time in oak barrels, adding some subtle fattiness and vanilla and spice notes to the wine.

The regions in the sidebar produce well-balanced, medium-bodied and smooth white wines.

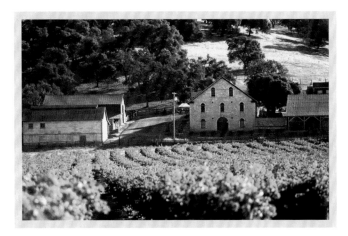

REGIONS

CHARDONNAY
Argentina
Canada (British Columbia, Ontario)
Chile
France (Burgundy)
Italy (Northern)
South Africa
United States
(Northern California, Oregon, Washington State)

CHENIN BLANC
Canada (British Columbia, Ontario)
Chile
France (Loire)
South Africa
United States (California)

PINOT BLANC
Austria
Canada (British Columbia, Ontario)
France (Alsace)
Italy

PINOT GRIGIO
Canada (Ontario)
Italy (Northern, Central)

PINOT GRIS
Canada (British Columbia, Ontario)
Switzerland

SÉMILLON
Australia
France (Bordeaux)

SÉMILLON/CHARDONNAY
Australia

OTHERS
Dry Gewürztraminer – France (Alsace)
Dry Vouvray – France (Loire)
Sancerre – France (Loire)
Soave Classico – Italy (Veneto)

HARMONY CHART

Chardonnay

FOOD AFFINITIES

SEAFOOD	MEAT POULTRY	HERBS SPICES	SAUCES	CHEESE NUTS	VEGETABLES FRUITS PASTAS GRAINS
Catfish	Chicken (roasted)	Chinese five spice	Chicken stock	Almonds	Asian pears
Shrimp in lemon	Pork	Garam masala	Cream (light)	Baker's cheese	Broccoli
Snapper	Turkey breast		Fish stock	Bocconcini	Corn
Sole	Veal		White wine	Caciotta	Lemons
				Fior di latte	Lettuces
				Havarti	Mushrooms (button, oyster, portobello, shiitake)
				Mozzarella	
				Oka	Onions
				Provolone	Spaghetti squash
				Scamorza	Semolina pasta
				Swiss	Zucchini
				Trecce	

FOOD CHALLENGES

SEAFOOD	MEAT POULTRY	HERBS SPICES	SAUCES	CHEESE NUTS	VEGETABLES FRUITS PASTAS GRAINS
Lobster	Red meat	Chilies	Barbecue	Blue-veined cheeses	Most fruits
Scallops		Ginger (dried)	Cream (heavy)	Brie (ripened)	Sweet potatoes
		Heavy pepper	Hoisin	Camembert (aged)	Winter squash
		Lemon rind	Red wine		

BEST METHODS OF PREPARATION
Grilling, roasting

BEST SEASONS
Spring, summer

COMPLEMENTARY CUISINES
Mediterranean

IDEAL OCCASIONS
Barbecue, picnic

Tuscan White Bean Bruschetta

SERVES 4

With Tuscan simplicity in mind, this bruschetta tastes best
with fresh garlic, fresh Italian bread and fresh mozzarella.

1 cup	250 mL	cooked white beans
2 Tbsp	25 mL	fresh lemon juice
		salt and pepper to taste
8	8	slices Italian bread
2	2	cloves garlic
1/4 cup	50 mL	finely chopped fresh Italian parsley
1 lb	500 g	fresh mozzarella cheese, carefully and thinly sliced

In a food processor or blender, purée beans and lemon juice
to a thick paste. Season with salt and pepper. Grill one side
of the bread slices until golden. Rub toasted side with garlic,
then spread with bean paste. Top with parsley and cover
with mozzarella. Grill until mozzarella is melted and bread is
golden on the bottom, about 3 to 4 minutes. Serve hot.

BUILDING BLOCKS

*The predominant building
blocks are the mozzarella's
subtle saltiness and lemon juice's
subtle sourness. A well-balanced,
medium-bodied, smooth white
with balanced sourness offsets the
subtle saltiness and works with
the lemon juice.*

FLAVORS

*Choose a well-balanced,
medium-bodied, smooth white
with toasty, earthy flavors to
match the white beans.*

Asparagus and Chèvre Flan

SERVES 4

This flan is great for brunch or lunch on a hot summer day with a side salad. When in season, you can use fiddleheads instead of asparagus.

1 lb	**500 g**	asparagus, trimmed

EGG MIXTURE

3	**3**	eggs
2	**2**	cloves garlic, minced
½ cup	**125 mL**	each half-and-half cream and chicken stock
2 Tbsp	**25 mL**	finely chopped chives
1 tsp	**5 mL**	honey mustard
½ tsp	**2 mL**	grated lemon rind
pinch	**pinch**	each salt, nutmeg, curry powder, black pepper
1 9-inch	**1 23-cm**	single-crust pie shell, uncooked
¼ lb	**125 g**	chèvre

Preheat oven to 325°F (160°C). In a steamer, steam asparagus until tender, about 5 minutes. Set asparagus in a bowl of ice water for 2 minutes. Dry on paper towels. In a large bowl, whisk together all the egg mixture ingredients. Evenly distribute asparagus in the pie shell. Cover with chèvre and pour egg mixture over cheese. Bake 30 minutes, until eggs are firm. Cool for 10 minutes before serving.

Zesty Wild Salmon Steaks

SERVES 4

Wild salmon is now available in many supermarkets. When cooking salmon, don't cook at too high a temperature or for too long. When salmon just begins to turn color but is still pink, remove from heat — the fish will continue to cook.

4	**4**	wild salmon steaks, 1 inch (2.5 cm) thick
pinch	**pinch**	cayenne
2 Tbsp	**25 mL**	olive oil
2	**2**	cloves garlic, crushed
¼ cup	**50 mL**	finely chopped fresh chives
¼ tsp	**1 mL**	grated lemon or orange rind
		juice from 1 lemon

Sprinkle salmon steaks lightly with cayenne. In a skillet, heat oil over medium heat. Sauté garlic until golden. Increase heat to medium-high and sauté steaks for 4 minutes on each side. Add chives and lemon rind. Sprinkle lemon juice over each steak. Cook 1 to 2 minutes longer. Arrange salmon steaks on a serving platter. Stir pan juices and drizzle over salmon.

FLAVORS

Choose a well-balanced, medium-bodied, smooth white with lemon flavor to match the lemon flavor in the drizzle.

Zucchini Polenta Tart

SERVES 4

This is a wonderful recipe, even for people who aren't zucchini fans. Even my husband, Jack, who once declared himself "not much of a zucchini guy," loves it.

2 1/2 cups	625 mL	water
1 cup	250 mL	cornmeal
		salt and pepper to taste
2 Tbsp	25 mL	olive oil
2	2	cloves garlic, minced
4	4	zucchini, sliced lengthwise
1 tsp	5 mL	fresh lemon juice
1 Tbsp	15 mL	finely chopped fresh basil
1/2 cup	125 mL	freshly grated Parmesan cheese

To make polenta, boil the water in a large pot and add the cornmeal in a very slow stream, stirring constantly. Reduce heat to low. Continue stirring in the same direction as the cornmeal thickens, 15 to 20 minutes. The polenta is done when it peels easily off the sides of the pot. Season with salt and pepper. Remove from heat.

Preheat oven to 350°F (180°C). Spray a 9-inch (23-cm) pie plate with non-stick cooking spray. In a large pan, heat oil over medium heat. Add garlic and sauté until aromatic. Add zucchini and lemon juice. Season with salt and pepper. Toss and sauté until zucchini is tender but not mushy, 10 to 15 minutes. Fold in basil.

Transfer slices of zucchini to pie plate, making sure they're flat and over-lapping. Sprinkle Parmesan over the zucchini. Spoon the polenta over the Parmesan, making a thick, even layer. Wet hands. Pat down polenta until flat. Smooth polenta hanging over the edge of the pie plate to make a crust.

Bake until polenta is golden, about 10 minutes. Run knife around edge of pie plate to loosen tart. Place glass plate upside down on top of pie plate and flip over. Let stand for 1 minute, then carefully remove pie plate. If tart doesn't come loose, bang bottom of pie plate. Serve hot.

BUILDING BLOCKS

The predominant building blocks are the Parmesan's subtle saltiness and the lemon juice's subtle sourness. A well-balanced, medium-bodied, smooth white with balanced sourness offsets the Parmesan and works with the lemon juice.

FLAVORS

Choose a well-balanced, medium-bodied, white wine with fruity, earthy, nutty flavors to match the lemony, earthy, nutty Parmesan. This style of wine also has a smooth, creamy texture that echoes the polenta's creamy texture.

BUILDING BLOCKS

The predominant building blocks are saltiness and fattiness from the bacon and sourness from the lemon juice and sour cream. A well-balanced, medium-bodied, smooth white with balanced sourness and subtle fattiness offsets the saltiness and works with the lemon juice, sour cream and bacon.

FLAVORS

Choose a well-balanced, medium-bodied, smooth white wine with toasty flavor to stand up to the rich, earthy flavors of the onion and bacon.

Onion and Bacon Tart

SERVES 4

This is my rendition of a traditional German onion pie that can be served as a side dish or as a luncheon dish with a side salad. The sour cream's tangy flavor contrasts nicely with the depth of earthy flavors in the onion and bacon.

4	4	thick slices bacon, diced
2 cups	500 mL	finely chopped onion
2	2	eggs, beaten
1 cup	250 mL	low-fat sour cream
1 tsp	5 mL	fresh lemon juice
2 Tbsp	25 mL	flour
		salt and pepper to taste
1 9-inch	1 23-cm	pie shell, parcooked
		paprika (as needed)

Preheat oven to 400°F (200°C). In a large skillet, fry bacon over medium heat. Remove from heat, drain on paper towel, then crumble. Drain most of fat from pan. Add onions and sauté over medium heat until tender. Set aside. In a bowl, beat together eggs, sour cream and lemon juice. Add flour and beat again. Season with salt and pepper.

Prick the pie shell several times with a fork. Spread the onions and bacon over the bottom. Pour the sour cream mixture over top. Season with paprika. Bake 15 minutes. Reduce heat to 350°F (180°C) and bake another 30 minutes, until top is golden. Serve hot.

Velouté Soup of Fiddleheads and Oka

SERVES 4

Freshly picked fiddleheads have an incredible woody flavor. You can actually taste the forest in them. This woody character works with the rich, creamy texture of Oka cheese. If fiddleheads are out of season, use fresh asparagus.

2 tsp	10 mL	butter
½	½	medium onion, diced
1 ½ cups	375 mL	fresh fiddleheads, washed, trimmed and steamed
2 tsp	10 mL	all-purpose flour
2 cups	500 mL	chicken stock
1 tsp	5 mL	fresh lemon juice
		salt and pepper to taste
¼ lb	125 g	Oka cheese, diced*
1	1	lemon, quartered (for garnish)

*Any soft ripened cheese can be used in place of Oka.

In a large saucepan, melt butter over low heat. Sweat onion for 2 to 3 minutes, until soft. Add fiddleheads and sprinkle with flour. Cook for 4 minutes, stirring constantly. Add chicken stock and lemon juice and season with salt and pepper. Simmer velouté gently for 20 minutes, stirring occasionally.

Strain velouté through a sieve and into a saucepan. In a food processor or blender, purée fiddleheads and onion, then stir into the velouté. Bring to a gentle boil. Gradually add Oka, stirring constantly until velouté thickens. Pour into heated soup bowls and garnish with lemon wedges. Serve immediately.

BUILDING BLOCKS

The predominant building blocks are subtle sourness from the lemon juice and subtle fattiness from the butter and cheese. A well-balanced, medium-bodied, smooth white with balanced sourness and subtle fattiness is a compatible partner.

FLAVORS

Choose a well-balanced, medium-bodied, smooth white with soft woody and nutty flavors to match the woody flavor of fresh fiddleheads and nutty flavor of the cheese. This style of wine also has a creamy, smooth texture that works with this soup's creamy base.

BUILDING BLOCKS

The predominant building blocks are sourness from the tomato and lemon juice and fattiness from the cheese, bacon and butter. A well-balanced, medium-bodied, smooth white with balanced sourness and fattiness is a compatible partner.

FLAVORS

Choose a well-balanced, medium-bodied, smooth white with some earthy flavor to match the earthy flavor of the onions and nutty flavor of peamale bacon.

Crustless Bacon and Tomato Quiche

SERVES 4

Seasoned cook Patti Peeters gave me my first experience of a crustless quiche. I've since fallen in love with crustless quiches. This is one of Patti's favorite recipes.

1 cup	250 mL	shredded cheddar
1/2 cup	125 mL	chopped spring onions
1	1	medium tomato, thinly sliced
1 tsp	5 mL	fresh lemon juice
6	6	thin strips cooked peamale bacon
		salt and pepper to taste
4	4	eggs
2/3 cup	150 mL	flour
1/3 cup	75 mL	melted butter
1 Tbsp	15 mL	baking powder
dash	dash	cayenne
1 2/3 cups	400 mL	milk

Preheat oven to 400°F (200°C). Spray a 9-inch (23-cm) pie plate with non-stick cooking spray. Layer cheddar, then onions, then tomato slices in the pie plate. Drizzle with lemon juice. Lay peamale bacon strips over tomato slices. Salt and pepper to taste. Set aside.

In a food processor or blender, blend eggs, flour, butter, baking powder and cayenne. Slowly add milk, blending until ingredients are well incorporated. Pour mixture over bacon. Bake 30 minutes or until center of quiche springs back and is golden. Do not overbake. Let stand for 7 to 10 minutes before serving.

Shrimp Wrapped in Chives with Tomato, Basil and Ricotta Sauce

SERVES 4

"Ricotta" means "cooked again." It is not actually a cheese, but a by-product made from the whey — water-soluble liquid — left over from the making of mozzarella and provolone cheeses.

12	12	chives
2 Tbsp	25 mL	butter
		juice from 1/2 lemon
24	24	shrimp, peeled and deveined
2 Tbsp	25 mL	finely chopped fresh basil
2 Tbsp	25 mL	white wine
1	1	clove garlic, minced
3	3	tomatoes, peeled and diced
1	1	shallot, minced
1/4 cup	50 mL	whole-milk ricotta
		salt and pepper to taste

In a pot of boiling water, blanch chives to soften, about 30 seconds. Drain and let cool. Cut chives in half lengthwise and spread them out wide. In a saucepan, melt the butter over medium heat. Add lemon and sauté shrimp and basil until shrimp are tender, about 2 minutes. Remove from heat and remove shrimp from pan. Roll a strip of chive around the center of each shrimp. Set on a plate seam-side down, cover and keep warm.

Return saucepan to medium-high heat. Deglaze pan with white wine, scraping up any brown bits. Add garlic and sauté until aromatic. Reduce heat to low and add tomatoes and shallot. Simmer until tender, about 1 minute. Add ricotta, stirring constantly until mixture is well blended. Season with salt and pepper. Carefully return chive-wrapped shrimp to saucepan and simmer gently for 2 to 3 minutes. On each plate, arrange 6 shrimp in a fan shape, surrounded with sauce. Serve very hot.

BUILDING BLOCKS

The predominant building blocks are subtle sourness from the lemon and white wine and subtle fattiness from the whole-milk ricotta. A well-balanced, medium-bodied, smooth white with balanced sourness and some fattiness is a compatible partner.

FLAVORS

Choose a well-balanced, medium-bodied, smooth white with lemon flavor to match the lemon juice and to work with the fruity flavor of tomatoes. This style of wine also has a smooth texture that works with the rich flavor of shrimp.

COOKING WITH WINE

A wine's quality, or lack thereof, will be revealed in the dish you're preparing. Stay away from cooking wines, thin wines and wines past their prime, all of which will give your dish a bitter taste. For excellent results, use only young wines with body and flavor.

Red and white wines are interchangeable in cooking. White sauces do need a white wine to retain the white color. Reds offer more depth of flavor and color, making them a better choice for heavier dishes with meat and game. Sweet wines work well in pastries and desserts, while those with a touch of sweetness enhance sweet meats, such as pork.

Add wine to a recipe according to its function. As a tenderizer or marinade, use it at the beginning of meal preparation. If the dish takes several hours to cook, add wine halfway through, so its qualities won't be lost. For a wine's aroma and flavor to predominate, add it at the end. Just be sure to add a little at a time. Above all, add wine to only one element of the meal. Otherwise, its wonderful effect will be lost.

BUILDING BLOCKS

The predominant building blocks are subtle sourness from the lemon juice and subtle fattiness from the chicken and olive oil. A well-balanced, medium-bodied, smooth white with balanced sourness and some fattiness is a compatible partner.

FLAVORS

Choose a well-balanced, medium-bodied, smooth white with some toasty flavor to work with the flavor of roasted garlic.

Roast Chicken with Lemony Garlic-Rosemary Crust

SERVES 4

As a non-taster and huge fan of excessive garlic, I love making this dish. Thank goodness my husband, Jack, is also a non-taster. Alter the amount of garlic based on the type of taster you are.

1	1	5-lb (2 1/2-kg) roasting chicken, neck and giblets removed
10	10	cloves garlic, crushed
1/2	1/2	small onion
3 Tbsp	45 mL	olive oil
2 Tbsp	25 mL	finely chopped fresh rosemary
1 Tbsp	15 mL	fresh lemon juice
		salt and pepper to taste

Preheat oven to 450°F (230°C). Rinse chicken under cold water and pat dry. Insert your fingers between skin and flesh to loosen skin, especially around breast and drumsticks. In food processor or blender, mince remaining ingredients. Place half the mixture under skin of breast and drumsticks. Spread remaining half on top of skin.

Place chicken, breast side up, in a broiler pan. Insert meat thermometer into meaty part of thigh, making sure not to touch bone. Bake 30 minutes, until meat is white. Internal temperature should be about 375°F (190°C). Remove from oven, cover loosely with foil, and let stand 10 minutes before serving.

Central American Chicken in Almond Sauce

SERVES 4

Ground almonds thicken the sauce, a traditional method used in both Mexican and Central American cooking.

¾ cup	175 mL	sliced almonds
4	4	boneless, skinless chicken breasts
pinch	pinch	salt
2	2	bay leaves
1	1	3-inch (7.5-cm) piece cinnamon stick
1 tsp	5 mL	dried oregano
2 Tbsp	25 mL	olive oil
3	3	slices bacon, chopped
2	2	cloves garlic, minced
1 cup	250 mL	chopped onion
1 tsp	5 mL	fresh lemon juice
1 cup	250 mL	chicken stock
		salt and pepper to taste
1 Tbsp	15 mL	finely chopped fresh Italian parsley

Preheat oven to 375°F (190°C). On a baking sheet, spread half the almonds and toast until golden, about 8 minutes. In a food processor or blender, grind remaining almonds until coarse — don't overgrind. Pat chicken breasts with paper towel to dry, and sprinkle with salt. Set aside.

In a skillet over medium heat, add ground almonds, bay leaves, cinnamon stick and oregano. Stir until almonds are golden. Do not let the skillet smoke. Transfer the mixture to a bowl and remove bay leaves.

In a clean skillet, heat oil over medium heat. Brown chicken on both sides, about 3 minutes. Remove chicken and add bacon. When bacon begins to brown, add garlic, onion and lemon juice. Fry for 3 minutes. Stir in ground almond mixture and chicken stock. Bring to a boil, then reduce heat to low. Add chicken breasts. Season with salt and pepper.

Let chicken simmer until white inside, 5 to 7 minutes. Remove from heat. Fold in parsley and toasted almonds. Discard cinnamon stick. Transfer chicken to plates and cover with sauce.

BUILDING BLOCKS

The predominant building blocks are subtle sourness from the lemon juice and subtle fattiness from the olive oil and chicken stock. A well-balanced, medium-bodied, smooth white with balanced sourness and some fattiness is a compatible partner.

FLAVORS

Choose a well-balanced, medium-bodied, smooth white with toasty, spicy flavors to match the flavor of toasted almonds and spicy flavor of the cinnamon.

BUILDING BLOCKS

The predominant building blocks are subtle sourness from the white wine and subtle fattiness from the cream. A well-balanced, medium-bodied, smooth white with balanced sourness and some fattiness is a compatible partner.

FLAVORS

Choose a well-balanced, medium-bodied, smooth white with lemon flavor to work with the fish flavor of clams. Wines within this style also have a smooth texture to match the creamy texture of this sauce.

BUYING AND CLEANING CLAMS

When shopping for fresh clams, stay away from ones that are already opened, chipped or damaged. Ask to have the clams packed in cool, fresh water. They breathe in the filtered, fresh water and push out salt water, in the process pushing sand from their shells. Within 20 minutes, they will have cleaned themselves. This helps reduce their natural saltiness. Be sure to also scrub the shells before incorporating them into your recipe.

Fettuccine with Baby Clams and White Wine

SERVES 4

Because clams are naturally salty, be conservative when seasoning the sauce. To have wine work with this dish, the wine's building block of sourness must predominate over the saltiness of the clams.

2 Tbsp	25 mL	butter
½	½	onion, minced
24	24	fresh baby clams, scrubbed and debearded
½ cup	125 mL	white wine
¼ cup	50 mL	Pernod*
3 cups	750 mL	half-and-half cream
		salt and pepper to taste
½ cup	125 mL	canned baby clams, drained and rinsed
1 lb	500 g	fettuccine

*Pernod can be replaced by ouzo or left out altogether.

In a large saucepan, melt butter over medium heat. Cook onion about 2 minutes. Add fresh clams and wine. Cover immediately and steam clams, shaking pot from time to time, 5 to 10 minutes. Once clams begin to open, remove cover and evaporate juice. Discard any that don't open.

Pour Pernod into metal ladle, flame it and pour over clams. Cook 1 to 2 minutes, over medium heat, until liquid has evaporated. Reduce heat to low, add cream and let simmer. Reduce liquid to desired consistency. Season judiciously with salt and season with pepper to taste. Add canned clams and cook gently until heated through, about 7 minutes. Keep warm.

Meanwhile, in a large pot of boiling, salted water, cook fettuccine until al dente, 7 to 10 minutes. Drain pasta and set in a bowl. Pour clam sauce over pasta, toss and serve hot.

Poached Wild Salmon with Cold Cucumber and Chive Sauce

SERVES 4

When chilled, the cold cucumber sauce is light and refreshing, contrasting nicely with freshly poached salmon steaks. The sauce can be served with a variety of fish and is also ideal for grilled salmon.

CUCUMBER AND CHIVE SAUCE

1	1	medium cucumber, peeled and puréed
1	1	clove garlic
1 Tbsp	15 mL	finely chopped fresh chives
2 tsp	10 mL	Dijon mustard
1 tsp	5 mL	each finely chopped fresh parsley and fresh lemon juice
3/4 cup	175 mL	mayonnaise

POACHING LIQUID

2 to 3	2 to 3	whole peppercorns
1	1	clove garlic, crushed
1	1	bay leaf
4 cups	1 L	fish stock or water
1/4 cup	50 mL	white wine
2 Tbsp	25 mL	fresh lemon juice
4	4	fillets wild salmon

To make sauce, place cucumber purée in strainer over a bowl and press with the back of a spoon to remove excess water. Reserve liquid. In a food processor or blender, combine garlic, chives, mustard, parsley and lemon juice. Pulse until ingredients are coarsely chopped. Combine with cucumber purée and mayonnaise, adding some reserved cucumber water to thin the mixture if necessary. Refrigerate for 1 hour.

To make poaching liquid, in a shallow pan large enough to hold the fillets, combine all the liquid's ingredients. Simmer on low, uncovered, for 25 to 30 minutes, taking care not to boil. Add salmon fillets and poach 9 to 12 minutes, until fish is firm to the touch. Arrange salmon on plates and pour sauce over top. Serve immediately.

BUILDING BLOCKS

The predominant building blocks are subtle sourness from the lemon and white wine and subtle fattiness from the salmon and mayonnaise. A well-balanced, medium-bodied, smooth white with balanced sourness and some fattiness is a compatible partner.

FLAVORS

Choose a well-balanced, medium-bodied, smooth white with lemon flavor to match the lemon flavor in the sauce, while complementing the fish flavor of the salmon.

BIG, **FAT** WHITES

PREDOMINANT BUILDING BLOCKS

- *Fattiness with some sourness and fruitiness*

FLAVORS

- *Buttery, creamy, oily, nutty, toasty, oaky and spicy; subtle fruity and floral flavors*

The factors that determine wines that fall into this style are the grape variety, the geography, climate and soil conditions of the wine region, and importantly, the winemaking techniques employed. The winemaker employs two predominant techniques to attain this rich, creamy texture and buttery flavor of big, fat white wines — malolactic conversion and barrel fermentation and barrel aging.

In most cool climates and some hot regions, winemakers put particular white wines through a secondary malolactic fermentation after the primary one. This converts some of the wine's aggressive and tart malic acid into the much softer, creamier lactic acid and produces diacetyl, experienced on the palate as a buttery flavor. This kind of bacterial fermentation doesn't always produce creamy texture and buttery flavor, however. The only way to know if a wine possesses these characteristics is to try it yourself or ask the wine merchant to recommend specific wines that fall into this style.

Wines produced in this style are also fermented and aged in oak barrels. Being porous, the wood slowly and gently exposes the wine to air, softening the tannins, toning down the acids and developing complexity in the wine's bouquet. Barrel fermentation and aging also adds extracts of butter, vanilla, spice, lactones and tannins to the wine — tannins that are different from those found in grape skins.

Once considered a fashionable wine style, the big, fat white has lost some of its luster — at least for some people. More than the other wine styles, big, fat whites harmonize with dishes containing butter, cheese and cream. So as far as I'm concerned, big, fat whites will always have a place in the culinary world as long as butter, cheese and cream exist.

Be careful when choosing wines in this style. Wine regions around the world make a variety of wine styles from one grape. Chardonnay, for example, can be produced in either a crisp, fruity or big, fat style, among others. The following regions are noted for producing big, fat white wines.

REGIONS

OAKED CHARDONNAY
Australia
Canada (British Columbia, Ontario)
Chile
New Zealand
South Africa
United States (California – Napa, Russian River, Sonoma)

OTHERS
Meursault – France (Côte de Beaune)
Pouilly-Fuissé – France (Burgundy)
White Burgundy (Premier Cru, Grand Cru) – France

HARMONY CHART

Barrel-Fermented and Barrel-Aged Chardonnay

FOOD AFFINITIES

SEAFOOD	MEAT POULTRY	HERBS SPICES	SAUCES	CHEESE NUTS	VEGETABLES FRUITS PASTAS GRAINS
Lobster	Bacon	Basil	Butter	Asiago	Avocados
Monkfish	Chicken	Chervil	Cream	Fontina	Corn
Mussels	Pheasant	Chives	Hazelnut oil	Hazelnuts	Fennel
Oysters (cooked)	Pork	Curry (mild)	Mayonnaise	Jack	Green cabbage
Salmon	Quail	Fennel seed	Velouté	Mozzarella	Green olives
Scallops	Rabbit	Garlic		Pecans	Mushrooms (chanterelles, porcini, shiitake)
Seabass	Sweetbreads	Ginger (mild)		Pumpkin seeds	Pasta (all)
Shark	Swordfish	Lemon peel		Sesame seeds	Polenta
Shrimp	Turkey breast	Mustard			Potatoes
Sturgeon	Veal	Nutmeg			Risotto
		Orange peel			Spinach
		Saffron			Sweet peppers (cooked)
		Sage (fresh)			White beans
		Tarragon			
		Turmeric			
		White pepper			

FOOD CHALLENGES

SEAFOOD	MEAT POULTRY	HERBS SPICES	SAUCES	CHEESE NUTS	VEGETABLES FRUITS PASTAS GRAINS
Anchovies	Beef	Cinnamon	Barbecue	Blue	Most fruits
Mackerel	Lamb	Coriander	Lime	Camembert	Artichokes
Sole	Squab	Dill	Salsa		Asparagus
Tuna		Rosemary			Green beans

BEST METHODS OF PREPARATION
Grilling, roasting, sautéing in butter

COMPLEMENTARY CUISINES
Canadian, French, Northern Italian

BEST SEASONS
Fall, winter

IDEAL OCCASIONS
Formal dinner

Grilled Potato Wedges with Garden-Fresh Herb Pesto

SERVES 4

This green pesto also works with pasta and as a pizza sauce.

4	**4**	medium potatoes, cleaned and thickly sliced
4	**4**	large cloves garlic, minced
¼ cup	**50 mL**	finely chopped fresh herb(s) of choice (such as basil, rosemary, oregano, parsley)
¼ cup	**50 mL**	olive oil

Place potato slices in bamboo steamer and par-steam for 5 minutes, until tender. Set on paper towel. In a food processor or blender, blend together remaining ingredients. Set aside. Grill potato slices on barbecue, 2 to 3 minutes per side, until golden. Top with fresh pesto and serve as appetizers.

BUILDING BLOCKS

The predominant building block is fattiness from the oil in pesto. A big, fat white is ideal.

FLAVORS

Choose a big, fat white wine with some grassy, herbal flavors to match the flavors in the pesto.

BUILDING BLOCKS

*The predominant building block
is fattiness from the butter,
chicken stock, cream and cheese.
A big, fat white is ideal.*

FLAVORS

*Choose a big, fat white with
toasty, spicy flavors to echo the
spicy flavor of peppercorns.*

Green Pea and Peppercorn Soup

SERVES 4

I've been making this soup for over a decade — it's always a crowd pleaser.

¼ cup	50 mL	butter
1	1	medium onion, chopped
1	1	large potato, cubed
2 cups	500 mL	frozen green peas
1 tsp	5 mL	green peppercorns
5 cups	1.25 L	chicken stock
¼ cup	50 mL	Chinese light soy sauce
2 Tbsp	25 mL	chicken bouillon powder
½ tsp	2 mL	each onion salt, celery salt and garlic salt
½ cup	125 mL	half-and-half cream
		bacon bits (for garnish)
		crumbled Asiago cheese (for garnish)

In a large pot, melt butter over medium heat and sauté onion until translucent. Add potato, peas and peppercorns and cook for about 3 minutes. Add chicken stock, soy sauce, bouillon powder, onion salt, celery salt and garlic salt. Bring to a boil and simmer, uncovered, over medium heat for 15 to 20 minutes, until potatoes are soft. In a food processor or blender, purée soup. Return to pot, add cream and simmer for 5 minutes or until heated through. Do not boil. Pour into soup bowls and garnish with bacon and Asiago.

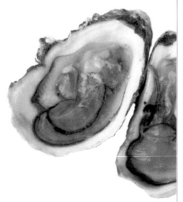

BUILDING BLOCKS

*The predominant building block
is fattiness from the bacon,
oysters and cream cheese. A big,
fat white is ideal.*

FLAVORS

*Choose a big, fat white with
toasty, smoky flavors to match
the smoky flavor of smoked
oysters.*

Piggyback Oysters

SERVES 4

I cannot count how many times I've made these little gems, and every time I do, people ask for the recipe. I obtained this recipe from Michelle Ramsay, with whom I wrote a previous cookbook.

½ lb	250 g	bacon
2	2	cans (4 oz/ 125 mL) smoked oysters
1 cup	250 mL	cream cheese

Preheat oven to 400°F (200°C). Cut each bacon slice in half. Place one oyster on each piece. Place a dollop of cream cheese beside each oyster. Roll up bacon and secure with a toothpick. Place bacon rolls on a greased baking sheet. Bake in the middle of oven for 10 minutes. Turn and cook another 8 to 10 minutes, until bacon is crisp. Drain on paper towel and serve hot.

Soup of Mussels, Leeks and Fresh Chervil

SERVES 4

Chervil is a springtime herb and has a natural affinity for other foods enjoyed in the spring, such as mussels, salmon, young asparagus, new potatoes and carrots.

2 Tbsp	25 mL	butter
1/3 cup	75 mL	diced leeks
2 cups	500 mL	fish stock
2/3 cup	150 mL	clotted cream
1	1	clove garlic, minced
2 Tbsp	25 mL	vermouth
2 Tbsp	25 mL	white wine
1 tsp	5 mL	finely chopped shallots
		salt and pepper to taste
15	15	mussels, scrubbed and debearded
3/4 cup	175 mL	Oka cheese, diced*
4	4	sprigs fresh chervil (for garnish)

*Oka can be replaced with any soft, ripened cheese.

In a large saucepan, melt butter over medium heat and sweat leeks until soft about 2 minutes. Add stock and simmer gently for 15 minutes. Strain stock, reserving the leeks. Return stock to the saucepan and bring to a simmer. Gradually stir in cream and reduce heat to low.

In another saucepan, combine garlic, vermouth, wine, shallots, salt and pepper over medium-high heat and bring to boil. Add mussels. Cover and steam for 3 to 5 minutes, until mussels open. Remove mussels with a slotted spoon, discarding any that are unopened. Remove mussels from shells. Keep warm. Strain mussel stock. Stir in cream stock and bring to a boil. Reduce heat to low. Whisk in Oka, stirring constantly until melted.

Place mussels in heated bowls. Distribute leeks evenly. Pour soup over mussels and leeks. Garnish with chervil sprigs.

BUILDING BLOCK

The predominant building block is fattiness from the butter, clotted cream and cheese. A big, fat white is ideal.

FLAVORS

Choose a big, fat white with toasty flavor to work with the subtle flavor of earthiness from the garlic and shallots. This wine style also possesses a creamy texture that works with the soup's creamy texture.

BUYING AND CLEANING MUSSELS

Do not buy chipped, broken or damaged mussels. Ask to have them put into a bag filled with clean, fresh water. The mussels will begin to clean themselves, expelling sand from their shells. Once home, remove mussels from the bag and wrap in a moist towel. If they're stored in plastic, it prevents them from breathing. Use them within a day.

When ready to use, scrub the shells under cool running water. To debeard them, grab the fibers and yank them out, tugging toward the hinged point of the shell.

Green Cabbage Soup with Two Cheeses

SERVES 4

While a bit fattening, this soup is ideal for winter dining. The original version, created by chef Christopher English, used four kinds of cheese. To reduce the expense and fat, I've cut the recipe to two.

4 cups	1 L	chicken stock
3/4 cup	175 mL	shredded green cabbage
2/3 cup	150 mL	diced potatoes
1/3 cup	75 mL	sliced onions
2 Tbsp	25 mL	butter
1/4 cup	50 mL	julienned leeks
3/4 cup	175 mL	half-and-half cream
2/3 cup	150 mL	heavy cream
1/2 cup	125 mL	fontina cheese, shredded
1/3 cup	75 mL	crumbled Asiago cheese
		clotted cream (for garnish)
		fresh mint leaves (for garnish)

In a stockpot, simmer stock, cabbage, potatoes and onions over medium heat until vegetables are tender, about 25 minutes. Meanwhile, melt butter in a saucepan over medium heat and sauté leeks until tender. Transfer leeks to stock. Bring stock to a boil. Stir in both creams and return to a boil, stirring constantly. Add cheeses and stir until completely melted. In a food processor or blender, purée soup in batches. Pour into heated bowls. Garnish with a dollop of clotted cream and fresh mint leaves.

White Bean and Escarole Soup

SERVES 4

While I was working on an article celebrating four main ingredients or less, caterer Jen Bird made this soup for me. It's so simple and delicious and works nicely with wine.

2	2	Italian sausages, casings removed
4 cups	1 L	chicken stock
1 cup	250 mL	cooked white navy beans
		salt and pepper to taste
1	1	bunch escarole, washed

In a skillet, brown sausage meat over medium heat until cooked and light golden, 7 to 10 minutes. Drain fat. Reserve meat. In a large pot, bring chicken stock to boil. Add sausage and navy beans. Season with salt and pepper and simmer for 15 minutes. Place 3 to 5 leaves of escarole in soup bowls. Pour soup over escarole. Serve hot.

Lobster-Stuffed Cabbage Rolls with Monterey Jack Sauce

SERVES 4

You can substitute artificial lobster or crabmeat made mostly of white fish for real lobster. The flavor of the cabbage rolls with the crabmeat is not as rich, but my husband actually prefers it to lobster.

1	1	head Savoy cabbage
1 Tbsp	15 mL	butter
1	1	shallot, minced
1 1/2 cups	375 mL	chopped lobster meat
2 Tbsp	25 mL	brandy
1/3 cup	75 mL	white wine
3/4 tsp	4 mL	paprika
1/3 cup	75 mL	fish stock
1/4 cup	50 mL	clotted cream
		salt and pepper to taste
1/2 cup	125 mL	shredded Monterey jack cheese

Remove tough outer leaves from cabbage and trim stalk. Tie cabbage with kitchen string to keep it whole while cooking. In a large bowl of lightly salted water, soak cabbage for 30 minutes. In a large pot of boiling, salted water, boil cabbage for 8 to 10 minutes, until outer leaves are tender. Drain and set aside to cool.

In a medium saucepan, melt butter over medium heat and sauté shallot until tender, about 2 to 3 minutes. Add lobster meat. Increase heat to medium-high and deglaze pan with brandy, scraping up brown bits. Add white wine and paprika. Simmer mixture gently until reduced by half. Add stock and simmer 2 to 3 minutes, until reduced by half. Remove from heat. With a slotted spoon, remove the lobster from sauce. Reserve sauce.

Preheat oven to 300°F (150°C). On your work surface, spread out 4 cabbage leaves, stem end toward you. Spoon lobster onto each leaf, about 1 inch (2.5 cm) from the stem end. Fold in sides and roll up tightly in jelly-roll fashion. Transfer rolls to a 9-inch (2.5-L) baking dish sprayed with non-stick cooking spray. Keep warm in oven.

Over high heat, bring sauce to a boil. Add cream, salt and pepper. Return to a boil, stirring constantly, then immediately reduce heat. Add cheese, stirring constantly until melted. Remove from heat. Arrange lobster rolls on plates and spoon sauce around rolls. Serve hot.

BUILDING BLOCKS

The predominant building block is fattiness from the butter, cream and cheese. A big, fat white is ideal.

FLAVORS

Choose a big, fat white with buttery, nutty flavors to match the rich flavor of lobster and nutty flavor of cheese. Wines within this style also possess a creamy texture that harmonizes with the creaminess of this sauce.

Potato Galettes with Wild Mushrooms and Thyme

SERVES 4

This galette is a heavy main course that can be served with a green salad. If you love garlic, use 3 or 4 cloves. Potatoes are hardy enough to hold as much garlic as your palate desires.

1 Tbsp	15 mL	butter
1	1	clove garlic, minced
1 cup	250 mL	diced oyster mushrooms
		melted butter (for coating parchment paper)
2 Tbsp	25 mL	butter
3	3	large potatoes, peeled, cut into 1/8-inch (0.3-cm) thick rounds
1 Tbsp	15 mL	finely chopped fresh thyme
		salt and pepper to taste

In a large skillet, melt butter over medium heat. Add garlic and mushrooms and sauté until tender, about 5 minutes. Remove from heat and let cool. Preheat oven to 450°F (230°C). Position rack in bottom third of oven. Spray two 9-inch (2.5-L) cake pans with non-stick cooking spray. Line bottoms with parchment paper and brush generously with melted butter. In another bowl, combine remaining butter, potato rounds and thyme. Season with salt and pepper. Toss.

In each pan, overlap a quarter of the potato rounds. Sprinkle a quarter of the mushroom mixture over potatoes in each pan. Repeat layers in both pans with remaining potatoes and mushroom mixture.

Bake galettes until potatoes are tender inside, crisp and golden outside, about 40 minutes. Remove from heat. Let stand 10 minutes before inverting onto platters. Peel off parchment. Cut into wedges and serve hot.

Asparagus and Havarti Tureen

SERVES 4

If in season, fiddleheads can be used instead of asparagus.

1 lb	500 g	fresh asparagus, trimmed
4	4	eggs
²/₃ cup	150 mL	half-and-half cream
2	2	cloves garlic, grated
1	1	small onion, grated
2 Tbsp	25 mL	finely chopped fresh chives
1 Tbsp	15 mL	baking powder
		salt and pepper to taste
1 cup	250 mL	shredded havarti cheese (or as desired)

Preheat oven to 350°F (180°C). In a steamer, steam asparagus until tender, about 5 minutes. Set in bowl of ice water for 2 minutes. Dry on paper towel. Set aside. In a blender, beat eggs with cream. Add garlic, onion, chives and baking powder. Continue to blend until slightly whipped. Season with salt and pepper.

Lay half the asparagus in a buttered 8-inch (2-L) square baking dish. Pour in half the egg mixture. Sprinkle with half the cheese. Repeat with remaining asparagus, egg mixture and cheese. Shred more cheese if desired.

Cover with foil and bake 20 minutes. Remove foil and continue baking for another 10 minutes, until the top is golden and eggs are set. Let sit 5 minutes. Serve hot.

BUILDING BLOCKS

The predominant building block is fattiness from the half-and-half cream and cheese. A big, fat white is ideal.

FLAVORS

Choose a big, fat white with some earthy flavor to work with the vegetal flavor of asparagus.

BUILDING BLOCKS

The predominant building block is fattiness from the butter, pastry and cheese. A big, fat white is ideal.

FLAVORS

Choose a big, fat white with buttery flavor to match the flavor of butter and work with the flavor of potatoes. This wine style also has a creamy texture that works with the creaminess of havarti cheese.

Puff Pastry Pie with Potatoes and Havarti

SERVES 4

Potatoes and cheese are a classic flavor combination. A delicate-tasting cheese, havarti adds weight and creaminess to any dish.

¼ cup	50 mL	butter
¾ cup	175 mL	julienned leeks
1 lb	500 g	frozen puff pastry
		flour (for dusting)
½ lb	250 g	potatoes, peeled and thinly sliced
½ lb	250 g	havarti cheese, sliced
		egg wash (1 egg yolk beaten with 1 tsp/5 mL water)
		salt to taste

In a large saucepan, melt butter over medium heat and sauté leeks until transparent, about 2 minutes. Set aside. Place puff pastry dough on a lightly floured work surface and dust with flour. Roll out into a rectangle 11 x 12 inches (28 x 30 cm) and ⅛ inch (0.3 cm) thick. Transfer dough to a lightly greased baking sheet. Cover and refrigerate at least 30 minutes.

Sprinkle potato slices with salt. Let dry. Fold chilled dough in half lengthwise on the baking sheet to make a seam, then open. Arrange potato slices, leeks and havarti slices on one half of the dough, leaving a ¾-inch (2-cm) border around edges. Brush border with egg wash. Fold other half of dough over filling. Press edges together with a fork, then trim with a pizza cutter. Lightly brush top of pie with remaining egg wash. Cut 3 steam vents in top. Refrigerate for 1 hour or until dough is firm and edges are well sealed.

Preheat oven to 400°F (200°C), then reduce heat to 375°F (190°C) and bake pie 20 to 25 minutes, until puffed and golden. Let cool 5 minutes before cutting. Serve hot.

Rigatoni with Baby Portobello Mushrooms and Toasted Pistachios

SERVES 4

I developed this recipe specifically for this wine style. It's rich and wonderfully fattening. One night I took a bowl over to my neighbors, who declared it, "Decadent!"

½ cup	125 mL	shelled pistachios
2 Tbsp	25 mL	butter
2 to 3	2 to 3	cloves garlic, minced
1 Tbsp	15 mL	finely chopped fresh rosemary
3	3	portobello mushrooms, thinly sliced
½ cup	125 mL	white wine
½ cup	125 mL	half-and-half cream
		salt and pepper to taste
1 lb	500 g	dried rigatoni
½ cup	125 mL	freshly grated Parmesan cheese

Preheat oven to 400°F (200°C). Sprinkle pistachios on baking sheet. Roast for 7 minutes or until toasted. Remove from baking sheet. Let cool for half an hour.

In a large skillet, melt butter over medium heat. Add garlic and rosemary and sauté until aromatic, about 2 to 3 minutes. Add mushrooms and sauté 2 minutes. Add wine and simmer another 2 minutes. Add cream. Season with salt and pepper. Cover and let simmer over low heat about 10 minutes. Meanwhile, in a large pot of boiling, salted water, cook pasta until al dente, 7 to 10 minutes. Drain and toss sauce with pasta. Sprinkle with Parmesan and toasted pistachios. Serve hot.

BUILDING BLOCKS

The predominant building block is fattiness from the cream. A big, fat white is ideal.

FLAVORS

Choose a big, fat white with toasty, nutty flavors to match the flavor of toasted pistachios.

NUTS AND WINE

When pairing wine with food, we rarely consider nuts. Yes, NUTS! Peanuts, almonds and others add flavor and texture to a variety of dishes. Here are some pairing suggestions.

- *Hazelnuts: Dishes highlighting hazelnuts and hazelnut oil work nicely with a big, fat white wine. Try marrying the toasty flavor of virgin hazelnut oil drizzled over barbecued salmon to a big, fat white with its own toasty flavor.*

- *Roasted peanuts: While unroasted peanuts are considered a basic Thai condiment, I prefer roasted, salted peanuts when marrying Thai dishes to wine. Ginger, cilantro, mild spice and salty peanuts sprinkled over a dish all harmonize with the hint of sweetness and crisp acidity in a chilled off-dry rosé.*

- *Walnuts: Dishes sprinkled with walnuts work well with an austere red because the tannin in both is astringent and makes the mouth dry. Drizzle a salad with vinaigrette made with soy sauce instead of vinegar and add fresh herbs and walnuts — you've got the perfect partner for an austere red wine.*

- *Macadamias: The crunchy texture and creamy flavor of macadamias harmonize with the creamy texture and oaky flavor of a big, fat white wine. Sprinkle roasted macadamias over a pilaf, and it's another dish altogether.*

- *Pecans: Entrées and desserts are enhanced by pecans and marry well to wine. There's nothing more delectable than ending a meal with dark chocolate truffles filled with caramel and pecans, served alongside a port-style wine.*

Grilled Chicken Pesto and Asiago Pizza

SERVES 4

When pairing pizzas to wine, use no more than five or six ingredients — a crust, sauce, two to three toppings and cheese. Too many cheese varieties or too many ingredients create muddled flavors.

1	1	pizza crust, parcooked (see page 126)
½ cup	125 mL	pesto (ready-made)
2	2	grilled chicken breasts, sliced into strips
½ cup	125 mL	shredded Asiago cheese
½ cup	125 mL	mozzarella cheese, shredded
3	3	slices tomato (for garnish)
		salt and pepper to taste

Preheat oven to 450°F (230°C). Spread pesto over pizza crust. Arrange chicken strips over the pesto. Sprinkle with Asiago, then mozzarella. Arrange tomato slices, overlapping, in center of pizza. Season with salt and pepper. Bake about 10 minutes, until crust is light brown and cheese has melted. Serve hot.

Grilled Chicken on Focaccia with Garlic-Parsley Mayo

SERVES 4

Considering its basic ingredients, this mayo has fabulous flavors. If you're a super-taster, you may want to cut back on the garlic.

4	4	boneless, skinless chicken breasts
		salt and pepper to taste
6	6	cloves garlic, minced
1 cup	250 mL	fresh Italian parsley
1 cup	250 mL	mayonnaise
8	8	thick slices focaccia, toasted
		lettuce of choice (as needed)

Season chicken breasts with salt and pepper. Grill on barbecue until meat is done, about 10 minutes. Keep warm. In a food processor or blender, purée garlic, parsley, mayonnaise and salt and pepper to taste until smooth and green. In a large skillet, simmer mixture over low heat, stirring constantly, for 5 minutes, until garlic is aromatic and sauce is heated through. Remove from heat. Generously spread mayo onto 4 slices of focaccia. Top with lettuce and chicken breasts. Place remaining focaccia slices on top. Cut and serve warm.

Pork Rouladen with Muenster

SERVES 4

"Rouladen" is German for "rolled-up meat." While easy to prepare, this recipe takes some time — it's a good one to make for weekend entertaining. Chef Thomas Dietzel created the original version over a decade ago.

4	**4**	lean pork schnitzels (¼ lb/125 g) each

STUFFING

1 cup	**250 mL**	spinach, blanched
1	**1**	egg white
½ lb	**250 g**	lean ground pork
1 tsp	**5 mL**	Dijon mustard
¼ tsp	**1 mL**	each salt and paprika
pinch	**pinch**	white pepper
¼ lb	**125 g**	Muenster, shredded
1 tsp	**5 mL**	caraway seeds
2 Tbsp	**25 mL**	vegetable oil
¼ cup	**50 mL**	white wine

SAUCE

½ cup	**125 mL**	clotted cream
¾ tsp	**4 mL**	Dijon mustard
		salt and pepper to taste

Using a mallet, pound pork schnitzels into very thin steaks. To make stuffing, squeeze out excess water from spinach. Chop coarsely. In a food processor or blender, blend egg white, ground pork, mustard, salt, paprika and pepper. Transfer to a bowl and fold in spinach, Muenster and seeds.

Preheat oven to 350°F (180°C). Place a quarter of the stuffing at one end of each pork steak. Roll up tightly to form rouladen, tying with string or securing with toothpicks. In an oven-safe skillet, heat oil over medium heat, then fry rouladen until golden on all sides, 4 to 5 minutes. Remove from heat. Pour wine into skillet and cover with foil. Roast for 15 to 20 minutes, until pork is white and cooked throughout. Remove from skillet and keep warm.

To make sauce, place washed skillet on medium heat. Add remaining ingredients. Stirring constantly, reduce to two-thirds. Spoon sauce onto plates. Place rouladen on sauce and slice each into 4 slices. Serve hot.

BUILDING BLOCKS

The predominant building block is fattiness from the pork, cheese, oil and cream. A big, fat white is ideal.

FLAVORS

Choose a big, fat white with apple flavor to work with the flavor of pork. Wines within this style also possess a creamy texture that works with the creaminess of the sauce.

Baby Lamb Stuffed with Spinach and Triple-Cream Brie

SERVES 4

While this dish requires time to prepare, it's easy to make and well worth the effort. Award-winning chef Zdravko Kalabrick developed the original recipe.

2	**2**	baby lamb loins (each 2 lb/1 kg with bones), bones and trimmings reserved*

STOCK

3 Tbsp	**45 mL**	each diced carrots, onions, celery and leeks
1 tsp	**5 mL**	tomato paste
¼ cup	**50 mL**	cognac
2 cups	**500 mL**	water
		salt to taste

STUFFING

1 cup	**250 mL**	spinach, blanched
3 oz	**85 g**	triple-cream brie
1 Tbsp	**15 mL**	finely chopped fresh tarragon
		salt and pepper to taste
		olive oil (for rubbing)
2 Tbsp	**25 mL**	olive oil

SAUCE

1 Tbsp	**15 mL**	vegetable oil
2	**2**	shallots, chopped
¼ cup	**50 mL**	white wine
¼ cup	**50 mL**	clotted cream
3 oz	**85 g**	triple-cream brie, cubed

*If possible, choose baby lamb under 3 months old.

Preheat oven to 450°F (230°C). To make stock, in a 9-inch (2.5-L) roasting pan, roast lamb bones until burned, about 1 ½ hours. Add diced vegetables and cook for another 20 to 30 minutes. Transfer bones and vegetables to a large saucepan and stir in tomato paste. Set roasting pan over high heat and deglaze with cognac, scraping up brown bits. Set aside roasting pan. Pour this liquid, then the water over the bones. Bring stock to a boil. Reduce heat and simmer, covered, for 2 hours. Season with salt. Strain stock through a sieve and set aside.

To make stuffing, in a food processor or blender, purée lamb trimmings, spinach, brie, tarragon, salt and pepper. In the top of each lamb loin, cut an incision 2 inches (5 cm) long and as deep as possible. Fill a piping bag (or plastic bag with a small hole in one corner) with stuffing. Using a wooden spoon to hold open the incision, pipe stuffing into each loin. Tie loins with kitchen string to keep stuffing in place. Rub olive oil lightly over loins.

Preheat oven to 375°F (190°C). In a large skillet, heat olive oil over medium heat and brown loins on all sides, about 90 seconds each side. Arrange loins in the roasting pan and roast for 5 minutes for rare, 15 minutes for well done. Keep warm.

To make the sauce, in the large washed skillet, heat oil over medium heat and sauté shallots until soft, about 2 to 3 minutes. Increase heat to medium-high and add wine. Pour in reserved stock and boil until reduced by half. Stir in cream. Simmer until reduced by one-quarter. Remove from heat. Add brie, stirring constantly until melted. Strain sauce through a strainer. Remove string from loins. Slice into medallions and arrange on serving plates. Spoon sauce around the lamb.

Oka and Summer Sausage Pancakes

SERVES 4

Oka is a semi-soft, washed-rind cheese with a mild butter texture and flavors of nuts and fruit. Use Oka made from pasteurized milk. You can also use other semi-soft cheeses, such as Taleggio.

PANCAKE BATTER

1 Tbsp	15 mL	butter
1	1	green onion, chopped
2	2	eggs
1 cup	250 mL	each all-purpose flour and milk
¼ cup	50 mL	summer sausage, finely diced*
1 tsp	5 mL	each baking powder, fresh lemon juice and Worcestershire sauce
½ tsp	2 mL	each salt and pepper
½ lb	250 g	Oka cheese, shredded

*Other mild sausages can be substituted.

In a large non-stick skillet, melt butter over medium heat and sauté green onion until slightly transparent, about 2 minutes. In a bowl, combine green onion with remaining batter ingredients. Stir until smooth.

Using same skillet, spoon 3 Tbsp (45 mL) batter for each pancake. Cook pancakes for 2 to 3 minutes, until tiny air bubbles form. Flip pancakes over and cook on other side for 1 minute, until golden. Transfer to baking sheet sprayed with non-stick cooking spray. Sprinkle each with cheese and broil until cheese is slightly melted. Be careful not to burn the pancakes.

BUILDING BLOCKS

The predominant building block is fattiness from the butter, sausage and cheese. A big, fat white is ideal.

FLAVORS

Choose a big, fat white with fruity, nutty, toasty flavors to match the nutty, earthy flavors of Oka.

Phyllo-Wrapped Chicken Breasts with Ripened Brie and Walnuts

SERVES 4

This dish offers a variety of textures — the crisp pastry, firm chicken, crunchy walnuts and velvety sauce.

FILLING

1	1	slice white bread, crust removed, diced
½ cup	125 mL	diced ripened brie
3 Tbsp	45 mL	each chopped walnuts and white wine
pinch	pinch	pepper
4	4	boneless, skinless chicken breasts
16	16	sheets phyllo pastry
3 Tbsp	45 mL	butter, melted

SAUCE

1	1	shallot, sliced
1	1	clove garlic, sliced
1 cup	250 mL	white wine
1 cup	250 mL	half-and-half cream
½ cup	125 mL	diced ripened brie
		salt and pepper to taste

Preheat oven to 325°F (160°C). In a bowl, mix together all the filling ingredients. In each breast, cut a pocket 2 inches (5 cm) long and ¼ inch (0.5 cm) deep. Stuff each pocket with a quarter of the filling.

On your work surface, lay out a phyllo sheet and brush with melted butter. Top with another sheet and brush with butter. Repeat until 4 sheets have been used. Place a stuffed breast at one end of the pastry sheet. Fold in sides and roll until the breast is wrapped in pastry. Repeat for remaining breasts. Place wrapped breasts on a baking sheet sprayed with non-stick cooking spray. Brush lightly with butter. Bake 15 to 20 minutes, until phyllo is golden and crispy. Keep warm.

To make sauce, in a medium saucepan, combine shallot, garlic and wine over medium heat and reduce to one-quarter. Stir in cream and reduce by half. Reduce heat to low. Stirring constantly, slowly add brie until melted. Strain sauce through a sieve. Return to saucepan. Season with salt and pepper. Reheat. Spoon sauce onto plates and set wrapped breasts on top. Slice each into 4 slices.

Racks of Lamb with Four Cheeses

SERVES 4

Rack of lamb is a great alternative to beef.

4	4	racks lamb (1/2 lb/250 g each), or consisting of 5 ribs, trimmed and cut country-style*

STUFFING

1/3 cup	75 mL	Swiss chard, blanched
1/4 lb	125 g	feta cheese, diced
1/4 cup	50 mL	pitted kalamata olives, chopped (in oil)
3 oz	85 g	bocconcini cheese, diced
1/4 tsp	1 mL	each salt and finely chopped fresh rosemary
		salt and pepper to taste

SAUCE

1	1	roasted red pepper, seeded and peeled
3 Tbsp	45 mL	ricotta
1 Tbsp	15 mL	grated Romano cheese
		salt and pepper to taste
4	4	sprigs fresh rosemary (for garnish)

*Ask your butcher to trim and cut country-style.

Preheat oven to 325°F (160°C). Open lamb racks away from ribs. Using a mallet, pound meat until flat. To make stuffing, gently squeeze out excess water from Swiss chard and chop coarsely. In a bowl, combine all the stuffing ingredients. Spread a quarter of the stuffing along ribs of each rack. Fold over meat and secure to ribs with kitchen string. On baking sheet, roast 30 to 35 minutes or until medium rare. Keep warm.

In a food processor or blender, purée red pepper. With motor running, add ricotta and Romano. Season with salt and pepper. Transfer to a saucepan and warm sauce over medium heat. Cut lamb racks into ribs. Lay a circle of sauce on each plate and place a loin on top. Garnish with rosemary.

BUILDING BLOCKS

The predominant building block is fattiness from the four cheeses. A big, fat white is ideal.

FLAVORS

Choose a big, fat white with apple and toasty character to match the fruity flavor of feta and roasted flavor of red pepper.

STORING FRESH CHEESES

To help preserve the shelf life of fresh cheeses, such as bocconcini and ricotta, store the containers upside down in the refrigerator. This keeps the surface air inside the container from developing bacteria too quickly.

OFF-DRY WHITES

PREDOMINANT BUILDING BLOCKS

• *Balance of sourness and fruitiness with some sweetness*

FLAVORS

• *Tropical citrus and hard fruits; floral notes, such as roses; minerals, nutty and spicy tones*

Some believe that sweet wines are for those with an uneducated palate. This is untrue. While dry white wines have become more fashionable, this does not mean we should refrain from drinking wines with a hint of sweetness. Wines within this style complement endless spicy ethnic dishes. In fact, this style has become one of my favorites.

The factors that determine wines that fall into this style are the grape variety, the geography, climate and soil conditions of the wine region, and the winemaking techniques employed. In the making of off-dry white wines, the juice is fermented in stainless steel tanks, which allows the resulting wine to retain its crisp acidity. The juice is fermented until it reaches a desired alcohol level. At this point, the winemaker arrests fermentation, allowing the wine to retain some of its natural sweetness from the grapes.

A combination of techniques is used to arrest fermentation, such as the wine being rapidly chilled and treated with sulfur dioxide, or sorbate being added to the wine to kill yeast activity. The wine then undergoes a sterile filtration to remove all remaining yeasts before bottling.

The grape regions above right are stylistically noted for producing off-dry white wines.

REGIONS

RIESLING
Canada (British Columbia, Ontario)
Germany

GEWÜRZTRAMINER
Canada (British Columbia, Ontario)
France (Alsace)
Germany

COLOMBARD
Australia
United States (California)

OTHERS
Sylvaner – France (Alsace)
Müller-Thurgau – Germany

HARMONY CHART

Off-Dry Riesling

FOOD AFFINITIES

SEAFOOD	MEAT POULTRY	HERBS SPICES	SAUCES	CHEESE NUTS	VEGETABLES FRUITS PASTAS GRAINS
Catfish	Chicken	Anise pepper	Citrus	Most cheeses	Beets
Scallops	Pork	Black carda- mom pods	Hoisin		Blood oranges
		Black pepper- corns	Honey mustard		Cantaloupes
		Cinnamon	Mayonnaise (chipotle, jalapeño, pesto)		Carrots
		Cloves			Clementines
		Coriander seeds			Grapefruit (pink)
		Cumin seeds			Lemons
		Fennel seeds			Limes
		Fenugreek seeds			Mangoes
		Ginger			Mushrooms (chanterelles, porcini, shiitake)
		Green carda- mom pods			Onions
		Kaffir lime leaves			Oranges
		Kebasa			Papayas
		Lemon grass			Sweet potatoes
		Loomi			Winter squash
		Mace			
		Star anise			
		Sumac			

FOOD CHALLENGES

SEAFOOD	MEAT POULTRY	HERBS SPICES	SAUCES	CHEESE NUTS	VEGETABLES FRUITS PASTAS GRAINS
Mackerel	Game	Cinnamon	Barbecue	Blue	Artichokes
Oysters (raw)	Red meat	Coriander	Lime	Camembert	Asparagus
Sardines		Dill	Red wine		
		Rosemary	Salsa		

BEST METHODS OF PREPARATION
Barbecue, roasting

COMPLEMENTARY CUISINES
African, Asian, Indian, Jamaican, Thai, Moroccan

BEST SEASONS
Summer, fall

IDEAL OCCASIONS
Barbecue, picnic

Mayan Hot and Sour Chicken Soup

SERVES 4

This recipe is great when first made, but it tastes even better when refrigerated overnight and heated up the next day. Overnight, the flavors meld together nicely.

1	1	whole chicken, cut up into parts
5	5	cups chicken stock
		salt and pepper to taste
4	4	cloves garlic, minced
1	1	jalapeño chili, diced
¼ cup	50 mL	rice vinegar (or as desired)
1 Tbsp	15 mL	dried oregano
2	2	carrots, sliced
1	1	medium yellow onion, sliced
½	½	bell pepper, sliced

In a large pot, bring stock to a boil. Salt and pepper the chicken pieces. In a skillet, brown chicken over medium heat for 3 to 5 minutes. Add chicken pieces, skin removed, to stock and boil for 10 to 15 minutes. Add garlic, chili, vinegar, oregano and salt and pepper to taste. Reduce heat and simmer for 5 to 10 minutes. Add vegetables. Simmer another 15 minutes. Serve hot.

BUILDING BLOCKS

The predominant building block is hot and spicy from the chili. An off-dry white with some sweetness offsets the spiciness.

FLAVORS

Choose an off-dry white with some grassy flavor to bring out the subtle flavor of the oregano.

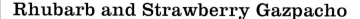

BUILDING BLOCKS

The predominant building blocks are fruitiness and sweetness from the strawberries and rhubarb. An off-dry white with some sweetness works with the strawberries and rhubarb.

FLAVORS

Choose an off-dry white with lemon flavor to match the flavor of lemon juice, while working with the flavors of strawberries and rhubarb.

Rhubarb and Strawberry Gazpacho

SERVES 4

One strawberry season, I picked my own fresh, ripe strawberries, came home and developed this cold soup. The rhubarb adds some sourness that harmonizes with the sourness of the strawberries.

1 cup	250 mL	off-dry white wine
		juice from 1/2 lemon
2 Tbsp	25 mL	sugar
4 cups	1 L	chopped fresh strawberries
1/2 cup	125 mL	diced rhubarb
1 tsp	5 mL	vanilla extract
		sour cream (for garnish)
		fresh mint leaves (for garnish)

In a large pan, combine wine, lemon juice and sugar. Boil over high heat, stirring occasionally, until reduced by half. Transfer mixture to a bowl. Let cool. In a food processor or blender, purée wine mixture, strawberries, rhubarb and vanilla. Transfer to a large bowl. Refrigerate, covered, for 2 hours, until well chilled. Ladle gazpacho into bowls. Garnish with a dollop of sour cream and mint.

FRESH FRUIT AND OFF-DRY WHITES

Wines with some sweetness (off-dry versions) and fruit-based savory dishes are harmonious companions. The wine's sweetness complements the natural sugars in the fruit. The key is to make sure the wine has more sweetness than the dish. Otherwise, the wine will taste sour, despite its level of sweetness.

Once you've built the foundation of your partnership of wine and food, which in this case is sweetness, look at matching or offsetting flavors. An off-dry white wine with citrus character works wonderfully with dishes highlighting citrus fruit, such as oranges or grapefruits. If the wine has tropical character, try a dish with tropical fruit flavors, such as mango or melon. Off-dry white wines are great partners for salads containing fresh fruit or cheese trays with fresh fruit.

Coconut Beer Shrimp with Lime Dipping Sauce

SERVES 4

Every chef offers a unique version of dipping sauce for coconut beer shrimp, but I prefer this lighter spicy lime sauce. Serve as a hardy appetizer or as a meal with a side dish.

LIME DIPPING SAUCE

		juice from 1 lime
¼ cup	50 mL	Chinese light soy sauce
½ tsp	2 mL	chili paste with fried garlic* (or as desired)
8	8	jumbo shrimp, peeled and deveined

SEASONINGS

1 Tbsp	15 mL	each black pepper, garlic powder, dried thyme, dried oregano

BATTER

2	2	eggs
2 cups	500 mL	flour
¾ cup	175 mL	ale (or as needed)
1 Tbsp	15 mL	baking powder
3 cups	750 mL	shredded coconut (unsweetened)
		vegetable oil (for deep-frying)

*You can find chili paste with fried garlic in Asian supermarkets. To make your own, add 2 to 3 minced garlic cloves to regular chili paste or dried pepper flakes.

In a small bowl, combine dipping sauce ingredients. Cover with plastic wrap and chill until needed. In a pot of boiling, salted water, parcook the shrimp about 1 minute. Do not overcook. Dry on paper towel. In a small bowl, combine the seasonings. Set aside. In a medium bowl, beat batter ingredients until smooth and not too thick. Place coconut in another bowl.

Coat each shrimp in seasoning, then dip into the batter and roll in coconut. Set on a plate. Cover with plastic wrap and refrigerate for 30 minutes. Heat oil. Deep-fry the shrimp for about 1 minute or until golden — watch carefully. Drain shrimp on paper towel. Serve hot with dipping sauce.

BUILDING BLOCKS

The predominant building blocks are fruitiness and sweetness from the coconut and hot and spiciness from the chili. An off-dry white with some sweetness works with the coconut and offsets the hot and spicy flavor.

FLAVORS

Choose an off-dry white with pineapple flavor to work with the lime and coconut flavors.

BUILDING BLOCKS

The predominant building blocks are fruitiness and sweetness from the banana and spiciness from the chili paste. An off-dry white wine with some sweetness works with the banana and offsets the spiciness.

FLAVORS

Choose an off-dry white with pineapple, mango and tropical flavors to work with the flavor of bananas.

Barbecued Oysters with Spicy Banana Salsa

SERVES 4

This is just another way for oyster lovers to indulge.

BANANA SALSA

1 tsp	5 mL	sesame oil
2	2	large bananas, peeled and cubed
1/2 cup	125 mL	diced golden raisins
2 Tbsp	25 mL	finely chopped fresh cilantro
1 Tbsp	15 mL	fresh lime juice
1 tsp	5 mL	oyster sauce*
1/4 tsp	1 mL	chili paste (or as desired)
		salt and pepper to taste
16	16	oysters in shells, about 4 inches (10 cm) long, scrubbed and shucked

*Oyster sauce is available at Asian supermarkets and sometimes in the ethnic food section of Western supermarkets.

To make banana salsa, heat oil in frying pan. Add banana and fry until golden, about 5 minutes. Transfer to a bowl. Let cool. Fold in remaining salsa ingredients. Start barbecue. Shuck oysters and spoon an equal portion of banana salsa onto each oyster. Set oysters in shells on the grill on low heat and cook until juices bubble, about 4 minutes. Serve hot in shells.

BUYING, STORING AND SHUCKING OYSTERS

When buying oysters, avoid ones with broken or damaged shells. Their shells should be closed or close when tapped and should smell clean, like the ocean. Once home, keep the oysters cup side down (flat side up) so that they will continue to live in their own liquid. They will die if stored in fresh water or in a closed plastic bag.

To shuck an oyster, place shell, cup side down, on a heavy towel. Grip curved end of shell with the towel and hold oyster firm and level. Insert an oyster knife into the hinge, between the top and bottom shell, at the narrow end. If necessary, gently wiggle the knife. Slide along the underside of the top shell to cut adductor muscle and free oyster. Remove the top shell. Gently slide the knife under the meat to cut it free from the shell. Leave meat in the shell. Set on ice until others are shucked.

Barbecued Pork Parcels with Sweet and Sour Dipping Sauce

SERVES 4

A good friend of mine, chef David Franklin, shared this recipe with me years ago. I've since made it for everyone I know. The parcels are addictive little appetizers and always well received.

SWEET AND SOUR DIPPING SAUCE

3 Tbsp	45 mL	apricot preserve
2 Tbsp	25 mL	ketchup
1 Tbsp	15 mL	each Chinese light soy sauce and rice vinegar
1/4 tsp	1 mL	Asian chili paste (or as desired)
1 lb	500 g	ground pork
1/2	1/2	small onion, minced
2 tsp	10 mL	minced garlic
1 tsp	5 mL	sugar
Pinch	Pinch	each salt and freshly ground pepper
1 Tbsp	15 mL	cornstarch
3 Tbsp	45 mL	finely chopped fresh mint
		mini rice papers, 6-inch (15-cm) rounds*
		Boston leaf lettuce leaves for lining papers

*Rice paper can be purchased at Asian supermarkets.

To make dipping sauce, in a small saucepan, mix all sauce ingredients and simmer for 2 minutes. Remove from heat. Pour into a bowl, cover and chill until needed. Combine pork with onion, garlic, sugar, salt and pepper. Cover with plastic wrap and refrigerate at least 2 hours.

Put meat mixture in a food processor or blender, add cornstarch and process to a fine paste. Fold in the mint. (This may also be done in a mortar.) Form the meat paste into oval balls, about 3/4 inch (2 cm) long, and slightly flattened. Set meatballs on a vegetable grill. Set vegetable grill on barbecue grill and grill on low heat until meat is golden on all sides, about 8 minutes. Remove from heat.

Fill a large bowl with hot water. Soak a rice paper in water about 1 minute or until soft. Lay a lettuce leaf on rice paper. Add meatball, then roll and fold into a small bundle. Repeat for all meatballs. Serve with dipping sauce.

BUILDING BLOCKS

The predominant building blocks are fruitiness and sweetness from the apricot preserve and spiciness from the chili paste. An off-dry white wine with some sweetness works with the apricot preserve and offsets the spiciness.

FLAVORS

Choose an off-dry white with some herbal notes to work with the subtle flavor of mint in the meatballs.

Baked Ripened Brie with Mango

SERVES 4

Use fully ripened mangoes for this appetizer. The sweet, ripe flesh pairs nicely with the earthy, nutty flavor of ripened brie.

1	1	(1 lb/500 g) ripened brie cheese with rind
2 Tbsp	25 mL	apricot or peach preserve
2	2	mangoes, peeled and sliced
		crackers (as needed)

Preheat oven to 400°F (200°C). Cut the brie in half horizontally. Spread preserve evenly over cheese. Lay slices of mango on top. Place top half of cheese on fruit. Wrap cheese wheel in foil. Place on a baking sheet and bake 15 minutes or until cheese is runny. Serve hot with crackers.

Lobster and Mango Salad

SERVES 4

This is an interesting combination of flavors worth trying.

4	4	lobster, steamed and cooled
4	4	large ripe mangoes, peeled and pitted (reserve 4 half shells)
2 cups	500 mL	finely chopped fresh basil
1/4 cup	50 mL	mayonnaise
2 Tbsp	25 mL	fresh lemon juice
2 tsp	10 mL	Dijon mustard
pinch	pinch	salt
1 1/4 cups	300 mL	whipping cream
		basil leaves (for garnish)

Sever lobster heads from body. Using lobster cutters, cut off claws and set aside. Cut shell of body and remove meat. Cut meat into cubes and place in a mixing bowl. Cube mango and add to lobster meat.

In a food processor or blender, purée basil, mayonnaise, lemon juice, mustard and salt. Transfer to a bowl. Fold cream into purée. Fold basil mixture into lobster and mango. Divide between four mango half shells. Garnish with basil and a lobster claw.

Farfalle Pasta with Roasted Cumin and Black Pepper Vinaigrette

SERVES 4

This pasta contains many spices believed to be aphrodisiacs: cumin, black pepper, ginger, coriander and cayenne. Whether or not this dish inspires Cupid's arrows, it's a tasty combination, perfect for summer dining.

ROASTED CUMIN AND BLACK PEPPER VINAIGRETTE

1	1	fresh Thai green chili, chopped or ½ tsp (2 mL) cayenne
		juice from 1 lime
½ cup	125 mL	orange juice
½ cup	125 mL	finely chopped fresh cilantro or 1 tsp (5 mL) dried coriander
¼ cup	50 mL	mango juice
1 Tbsp	15 mL	roasted cumin seeds
1 Tbsp	15 mL	minced fresh ginger or 1 tsp (5 mL) dried ginger
1 Tbsp	15 mL	liquid honey
		salt and pepper to taste

SALAD

¾ lb	375 g	farfalle pasta
3	3	green onions, thinly sliced
2	2	tomatoes, chopped
1 cup	250 mL	cooked fresh corn
2	2	avocados, chopped (for garnish)

To make the vinaigrette, in a food processor or blender, purée all the vinaigrette ingredients. Transfer to a bowl, cover and refrigerate until needed.

In a large pot of boiling, salted water, cook pasta until al dente, 7 to 10 minutes. Drain and rinse under cold water. Add touch of olive oil to keep pasta from sticking together. Combine pasta with vinaigrette. Toss salad with onions, tomatoes and corn. Arrange salad on plates. Garnish with avocado. Serve immediately.

BUILDING BLOCKS

The predominant building blocks are fruitiness and sweetness from the orange and mango juices and honey and spiciness from the chili. An off-dry white with some sweetness works with the orange and mango juices and honey and offsets the spiciness.

FLAVORS

Choose an off-dry white with lemon-lime flavor to match the orange and lime flavors in the vinaigrette.

BUILDING BLOCKS

The predominant building block is spiciness from the chili flakes. An off-dry white with some sweetness offsets the spiciness.

FLAVORS

Choose an off-dry white wine with lemon flavor to work with the flavor of lemon grass and the fish flavor of shrimp, shrimp paste and fish sauce.

Spicy Shrimp Patties

SERVES 4 TO 6

These patties are flavorful enough to stand alone, but also go nicely with the lime dipping sauce on page 99.

1 lb	500 g	shrimp, peeled and deveined
5	5	peppercorns
4	4	shallots
4	4	cloves garlic
1	1	stalk lemon grass, bruised and chopped*
1	1	egg, beaten
1 cup	250 mL	thinly sliced green beans
1 Tbsp	15 mL	shrimp paste**
1 Tbsp	15 mL	fish sauce (or as desired)
½ tsp	2 mL	dried coriander
½ tsp	2 mL	dried chili flakes (or as desired)
½ tsp	2 mL	lime peel
		vegetable oil (for deep-frying)

*Lemon grass is available in Asian supermarkets and some Western supermarkets.

**Other seafood pastes, such as crab, can replace shrimp paste.

In a food processor or blender, mix together all ingredients, except for oil. When mixture is a fairly smooth paste, transfer to a bowl. Roll into small balls and flatten each. In a heavy pot, heat oil. Deep-fry patties for about 4 minutes, until golden. Serve hot.

BUILDING BLOCKS

The predominant building block is sweetness from the apples, maple syrup and honey mustard. An off-dry white with some sweetness works with these ingredients.

Cured Ham with Maple Syrup and Apple Glaze

SERVES 4 TO 6

A classic Easter dish, this ham recipe expresses traditional Canadiana cuisine because of the apples and maple syrup.

MAPLE SYRUP AND APPLE GLAZE

1	1	McIntosh apple, diced
¼ cup	50 mL	each dark maple syrup and white wine
3 Tbsp	45 mL	finely chopped fresh sage
1 Tbsp	15 mL	prepared honey mustard
1	1	cured ham (6 lb/2.7 kg)
		whole cloves (as needed)
1	1	McIntosh apple, sliced into thin rings

Preheat oven to 325°F (160°C). To make glaze, in a pot, combine all glaze ingredients over low heat. While glaze is simmering, insert cloves into ham. Place apple rings on skin of ham, using toothpicks to hold in place. Set ham in a roasting pan and place in oven uncovered. Bake 1 ¹/₂ to 2 hours, basting every 15 minutes. Pour remaining glaze over ham for last 30 minutes. Ensure ham is hot throughout when done. Let stand for 5 to 10 minutes before slicing.

Orange Roughy with Lemon-Maple Butter Sauce

SERVES 4

Lemon and maple syrup are classic ingredient combinations that taste absolutely scrumptious together. This butter sauce can be used on a variety of white fish.

LEMON-MAPLE BUTTER SAUCE

		juice of 1 lemon
1	1	bay leaf
1	1	clove
¼ cup	50 mL	dark maple syrup
3 Tbsp	45 mL	half-and-half cream
2 Tbsp	25 mL	butter
2 Tbsp	25 mL	butter
4	4	fresh orange roughy fillets
		sea salt and freshly ground white pepper to taste

In a saucepan, combine lemon juice, bay leaf, clove and maple syrup over medium heat. Reduce to one-quarter. Add cream and simmer for 1 minute. Remove from heat and whisk in butter. Discard clove and bay leaf. Keep sauce warm.

In a skillet, heat butter over medium heat. Season fillets with salt and pepper. Cook, one side only, for 6 minutes or until bottom of fish is crispy and top is opaque. Drain on paper towel. Arrange fillets on plates and drizzle with butter sauce.

BUILDING BLOCKS

The predominant building blocks are fattiness from the mayonnaise and spiciness from the hot pepper. An off-dry white wine with some sweetness works with the mayonnaise and offsets the spiciness.

FLAVORS

Choose an off-dry white with pineapple and mango flavors to complement the flavors of garlic, coriander and ginger.

NAPA CABBAGE

While any lettuce will do in this recipe, I use Asian cabbage. Napa cabbage, known in Chinese as wong nga bok, *has loose, light green leaves with a crunchy texture and sweet flavor. It is also high in vitamin C, vitamin A and potassium. When shredded, Napa cabbage is an alternative to lettuce as a base ingredient in salads. Like bok choy, it cooks in about 30 seconds when added to a stir-fry. Store in plastic wrap in the vegetable drawer of your refrigerator.*

Saigon Burgers with Lime-Jalapeño Mayonnaise on a Baguette

SERVES 4

This is another great way to use ground meat on the barbecue grill in the summer.

1 1/2 lb	750 g	ground chicken
2	2	cloves garlic, minced
2	2	green onions, finely chopped
1/4 cup	50 mL	finely chopped fresh cilantro
1 tsp	5 mL	each salt and minced fresh ginger
1/2 tsp	2 mL	grated lemon rind
		hot pepper flakes (as desired)
1	1	narrow baguette, cut into quarters and split in half horizontally

LIME-JALAPEÑO MAYONNAISE

1/4 cup	50 mL	mayonnaise (or as desired)
1 tsp	5 mL	fresh lime juice
1/4 tsp	1 mL	jalapeño hot sauce (or as desired)
		shredded Napa cabbage (as desired)
		thinly sliced English cucumber (as desired)

Carefully combine ground chicken, garlic, green onion, coriander, salt, ginger, lemon rind and pepper flakes. Form mixture into four even-sized, elongated patties that are $^3/_4$ inch (2 cm) thick. Grill patties over medium heat for 5 to 7 minutes per side, until cooked to desired doneness.

Meanwhile, grill cut sides of baguette until lightly golden. In a small bowl, combine mayonnaise, lime juice and hot sauce. Spread each baguette with mayonnaise. On each bottom piece, place cabbage, a patty, then cucumber. Finish with the top of the baguette.

Marinated Shrimp with Hoisin-Lemon Dipping Sauce

SERVES 4

Hoisin sauce adds an interesting twist to this dish. Because it's sweet, most people love the taste.

HOISIN-LEMON DIPPING SAUCE

		juice from 1 lemon
2 Tbsp	30 mL	hoisin sauce
1 Tbsp	15 mL	grated fresh ginger
½ tsp	2 mL	chili paste (or as desired)
1 Tbsp	15 mL	each sugar, Chinese light soy sauce and sesame oil
20	20	shrimp, peeled and deveined

To make dipping sauce, whisk together all sauce ingredients. Set aside. In a glass bowl, blend together sugar, soy sauce and oil. Cover and marinate shrimp for 20 minutes. Steam shrimp in a bamboo basket over boiling water for about 2 minutes, until flesh is firm and white. Serve in the basket with dipping sauce on the side.

SOY SAUCES, STIR-FRIES AND WINE

One of the predominant ingredients in the Asian stir-fry is soy sauce. When marrying stir-fries to wine, match the flavor level in the soy sauce to the heaviness of the vegetables and flesh to the density of noodles.

Soy sauces generally fall into two categories — Chinese and Japanese. The following table outlines the vegetables, noodles and wine styles that work best with each soy sauce.

SOY SAUCE	VEGETABLE	NOODLE	WINE TYPE
Chinese: Light	Summer vegetables (scallions, green peppers, tomatoes)	Thin ramen	Crisp, dry white
Chinese: Dark	Heavier vegetables (sweet potatoes, potatoes, onions, carrots)	Thick rice	Off-dry rosé
Japanese: Koikuchi, Usukuchi, Shiro	Ginger, garlic, mushrooms, onions, carrots	Thin rice, vermicelli	Off-dry white
Japanese: Tamari	Red cabbage, mustard greens, onions	Buckwheat, soba	Light, fruity red
Japanese: Saishikomi	Beets, parsnips	Udon	Red with forward fruit

BUILDING BLOCKS

The predominant building blocks are sweetness from the hoisin sauce and spiciness from the chili paste. An off-dry white with some sweetness works with the hoisin sauce and offsets the spiciness.

FLAVORS

Choose an off-dry white with lemon flavor to match the flavors of lemon and ginger in the sauce.

BUILDING BLOCKS

The predominant building block is spiciness from the red pepper flakes. An off-dry white with some sweetness offsets the spiciness.

FLAVORS

Choose an off-dry white with some herbal flavor to work with the flavors of fresh herbs in the pesto.

Planked Shrimp with Chimichurri Pesto

SERVES 4

The original version of this recipe calls for steak, but I prefer to use shrimp. The spiciness of the chimichurri pesto is delightful with shrimp and an off-dry white.

		untreated cedar or alder plank*

CHIMICHURRI PESTO

2	2	cloves garlic (or as desired)
1/2	1/2	large onion, chopped
1/4 cup	50 mL	each chopped fresh Italian parsley, cilantro and mint
3 Tbsp	45 mL	red wine
2 Tbsp	25 mL	olive oil
		crushed red pepper flakes (as desired)
		salt and pepper to taste
16	16	tiger shrimp, peeled and deveined

*Cedar or alder planks can be purchased at building supply stores and cut to fit your barbecue grill.

Soak plank in water for 2 to 4 hours. Meanwhile, to prepare pesto, purée all pesto ingredients in a food processor or blender. Set aside.

Heat barbecue on high heat. Set plank on the grill, close lid and grill for 5 minutes or until plank is lightly charred. Carefully turn over plank. Reduce heat to medium and place shrimp on plank. Cover and grill for 3 minutes, until cooked. Do not overcook. Serve with chilled chimichurri pesto.

Grilled Tuna with Spicy Strawberry and Yellow Tomato Salsa

SERVES 4

The strawberry and tomato in this refreshing salsa harmonize extremely well and complement the flavors of tuna. The salsa will also last a couple of days in the refrigerator.

STRAWBERRY AND YELLOW TOMATO SALSA

4	4	green onions, chopped
2	2	yellow tomatoes, chopped
		juice from 1/4 lime
2 cups	500 mL	chopped fresh strawberries
1/4 cup	50 mL	chopped fresh cilantro
1 Tbsp	15 mL	each olive oil and balsamic vinegar
		salt and pepper to taste
pinch	pinch	red chili flakes (or as desired)
4	4	tuna steaks
		olive oil (as needed)

To make salsa, combine all the salsa ingredients in a food processor or blender and coarsely chop. Chill at least 1 hour. Brush tuna steaks with oil and place on preheated grill. Grill, covered, over medium-high heat for 7 to 10 minutes. Turn steaks and grill 5 more minutes or until exterior is grilled and middle is desirable. Serve hot with chilled salsa.

BUILDING BLOCKS

The predominant building blocks are fruitiness and sweetness from the strawberries and spiciness from the red chili flakes. An off-dry white wine with some sweetness works with the strawberries and offsets the spiciness.

FLAVORS

Choose an off-dry white with apple flavor to work with the strawberry flavor.

The predominant building blocks are fruitiness and sweetness from the mangoes and spiciness from the cayenne, ginger and pepper. An off-dry white with some sweetness works with the mangoes and offsets the spiciness.

FLAVORS

Choose an off-dry white with pineapple and mango flavors to work with the flavor of mango and ginger.

Grilled Halibut with Mango-Ginger Sauce

SERVES 4

Halibut is one of my favorite fish. When purchasing, look for a fresh smell and firm flesh. Once home, rinse the fish under cool water, pat dry and cover with plastic wrap. Store in the refrigerator for up to 2 days.

4	4	halibut steaks
pinch	pinch	each freshly ground pepper, seasoning salt and cayenne

MANGO-GINGER SAUCE

2	2	mangoes, peeled and pitted
2	2	cloves garlic, minced
1 Tbsp	15 mL	each fresh lemon juice and Dijon mustard
1 tsp	5 mL	minced fresh ginger
dash	dash	Worcestershire sauce
		salt and pepper to taste

Rinse halibut in cold water and pat dry. (Leave the skins on to hold fish together on grill.) Season steaks with pepper, seasoning salt and cayenne. Grill on low heat for 15 minutes per side, until flesh is flaky. Keep warm.

Meanwhile, to make sauce, in a food processor or blender, purée the sauce ingredients. Pour into a saucepan and heat through on low heat. Do not boil. Arrange halibut on plates and pour sauce over top.

Roasted Winter Squash Risotto with Maple Syrup

SERVES 4

Use pure, dark maple syrup in a glass bottle. It has an intense maple flavor that harmonizes well with winter squash. The glass container allows the maple syrup to retain its true flavor indefinitely.

2 cups	500 mL	favorite winter squash (1 whole butternut, for example)
2 Tbsp	25 mL	butter, melted
		salt and pepper to taste
4 cups	1 L	chicken stock
2 Tbsp	25 mL	butter
2	2	cloves garlic, minced
½	½	onion, minced
1 cup	250 mL	arborio rice
2 Tbsp	25 mL	dark maple syrup

Preheat oven to 350°F (180°C). Spray baking sheet with non-stick cooking spray. Cut squash in half and discard pulp and seeds. Drizzle flesh with melted butter and season with salt and pepper. Lay squash flesh side down on baking sheet. Bake 20 to 25 minutes, until soft but firm. Let cool, then scoop flesh from skin. Dice and set aside.

Meanwhile, to make risotto, in a large pot, bring stock to a boil. Reduce to a simmer. In a saucepan, melt butter over medium heat. Add garlic and sauté until aromatic, about 2 minutes. Add onion and sauté until just tender, about another 2 minutes. Add rice, coating with butter mixture. Slowly add about ¼ cup (50 mL) stock to rice, stirring constantly until stock is absorbed. Continue adding stock until all stock is used. When rice is tender but liquid is creamy, add diced squash. Simmer 3 to 5 minutes. Fold in maple syrup. Season with salt and pepper. Serve hot.

BUILDING BLOCKS

The predominant building block is sweetness from the winter squash and maple syrup. An off-dry white with some sweetness works with the squash and maple syrup.

FLAVORS

Choose an off-dry white with honey or maple syrup flavor to match the flavor of maple syrup.

The predominant building blocks are sweetness from the sugar and spiciness from the cayenne. An off-dry white with some sweetness works with the sugar and offsets the spiciness.

FLAVORS

Choose an off-dry white with some spiciness to work with the flavors of allspice, nutmeg and cinnamon.

Planked Jamaican Jerk Chicken

SERVES 4

Jerk is the most famous cooking method of the Caribbean. In Jamaica, authentic jerk pork and chicken are smoked on grills set inside covered holes dug along roadsides. The aromas make your palate salivate.

untreated cedar or alder plank*

DRY RUB

¼ cup	50 mL	each sugar and salt
2 Tbsp	25 mL	each onion flakes, onion powder and dried thyme
2 tsp	10 mL	each salt, freshly ground black pepper and allspice
½ tsp	2 mL	each nutmeg and ground cinnamon
½ tsp	2 mL	cayenne pepper (or as desired)
4	4	boneless, skinless chicken breasts
		rock salt (as needed)

*Cedar or alder planks can be purchased at building supply stores and cut to fit your barbecue grill.

In a medium bowl, mix together all rub ingredients. Transfer to a plate. Dredge chicken breasts in rub. Set breasts on new plate, cover and refrigerate overnight.

Soak plank in water for 2 to 4 hours. Heat barbecue. Set plank on the grill and lightly sprinkle plank with rock salt. Set breasts on salt. Close lid and grill on low heat. The plank will begin to burn and steam, smoking the chicken. Cook for 10 minutes. Coat breasts with more dry rub. Close lid and cook another 15 to 20 minutes, until flesh is smoked throughout. Discard leftover rub that has touched raw chicken. Store leftover dry rub in a dark airtight container in the refrigerator for up to 3 months.

Chicken Breasts
with Blue Cheese and Grapes

SERVES 4

The wonderful thing about off-dry white wines is that they complement all types of cheeses, including blue cheese.

STUFFING

¼ lb	125 g	havarti cheese, shredded
3 oz	85 g	baked focaccia bread, cubed
¼ cup	50 mL	coarsely chopped pecans
2 Tbsp	25 mL	finely chopped fresh thyme
¼ tsp	1 mL	salt
pinch	pinch	white pepper

CHICKEN BREASTS

4	4	boneless, skinless chicken breasts
		salt and pepper to taste
2 Tbsp	25 mL	butter
¼ cup	50 mL	white wine

SAUCE

1	1	medium shallot, sliced
1 cup	250 mL	white wine
1 cup	250 mL	whipping cream
½ cup	125 mL	crumbled blue cheese
16	16	small red seedless grapes (for garnish)

Preheat oven to 325°F (160°C). To make stuffing, in a medium bowl, mix together all the stuffing ingredients. In each chicken breast, cut a pocket 2 inches (5 cm) long and ¼ inch (0.5 cm) deep. Stuff each pocket with a quarter of the stuffing. Season with salt and pepper. Butter a roasting pan. Place breasts in the pan, pocket side up. Pour wine over them. Roast for 20 to 25 minutes, until breasts are white and tender. Keep warm.

To make sauce, in a medium saucepan, combine shallot and wine over high heat. Reduce to one-quarter. Reduce heat to medium and add cream and cheese. Stirring constantly, reduce by half. Spoon sauce onto plates. Set breasts on sauce and slice each into four slices. Garnish with grapes.

BUILDING BLOCKS

The predominant building blocks are fruitiness and sweetness from the grapes and fattiness from the cheese and whipping cream. An off-dry white with some sweetness matches the grapes and works with the cheese and whipping cream.

FLAVORS

Choose an off-dry white with lots of apple and pear flavors to work with the flavors of grapes and blue cheese.

OFF-DRY ROSÉS

PREDOMINANT BUILDING BLOCKS

• *Balance of sourness and fruitiness and some sweetness*

FLAVORS

• *Ripe, sweet berry fruit flavors, such as strawberry and cherry*

Rosé is generally produced in one of two ways. In direct pressing, red grapes are gently pressed, releasing a small amount of juice and little tannin and pigment from the skins. As a result, the wine is very pale, with fruity character and soft acidity and tannin. In bleeding, more color and tannin are imparted to the finished wine. Red grape skins are soaked for several hours in their juice, then the juice is drained off to make a pale red wine with good acidity and fresh, fruity flavors.

Off-dry rosés have the addition of some sweetness and so nicely offset a wide range of hot and spicy dishes. However, be sure to watch for sweetness level, as a wide range of off-dry rosés exist.

The regions above right are stylistically noted for producing off-dry rosé wines.

REGIONS

OFF-DRY ROSÉ
    Canada (British Columbia, Ontario)

OTHERS
    Mateus Rosé – Portugal
    White Zinfandel – United States (California)

HARMONY CHART

Off-Dry Rosé

FOOD AFFINITIES

SEAFOOD	MEAT POULTRY	HERBS SPICES	SAUCES	VEGETABLES, FRUITS PASTAS, GRAINS
Anchovies	Ham	Aleppo	Barbecue	Bell peppers
Shrimp	Prosciutto	pepper	Berry	Blood oranges
Tuna	Quail	Allspice	Hoisin	Carrots
	Sausage	Black pepper	Honey	Clementines
	Smoked	Caraway	mustard	Corn
	poultry/fowl	Grains of	Hot	Cranberries
	Turkey	paradise	Rosé	Fennel
		Star anise	Soy	Figs
			Teriyaki	Jicama
				Lemons

CHEESE NUTS

Almonds
Asiago
Parmesan

Limes
Mangoes
Melons
Mushrooms (all varieties)
Onions
Oranges
Papayas
Pears
Pink grapefruit
Raspberries
Strawberries
Sweet potatoes
Winter squash

BEST METHODS OF PREPARATION
Braising, grilling, roasting, smoking

COMPLEMENTARY CUISINES
Cajun, Chinese, Indonesian, Mexican,
Middle Eastern, Southwestern, Thai

BEST SEASONS
Spring, summer

IDEAL OCCASIONS
Barbecue, corn roast, picnic, turkey dinner
with cranberry sauce

FOOD CHALLENGES

SEAFOOD	MEAT POULTRY	HERBS SPICES	SAUCES	CHEESE NUTS	VEGETABLES FRUITS PASTAS GRAINS
Oysters	Squab	Dill	Butter	Blue	Apples
(raw)	Veal	Sage	Cream	Brie	Artichokes
Sole				(ripened)	Asparagus
Whitefish				Camembert	Bananas
				(aged)	Green
					beans
					Kiwi
					Pineapples
					Water-melons

Prairie Fire Buffalo Burgers

SERVES 4

Tim Belch, owner of Belch Farms, a buffalo farm near my home, gave me this recipe. Buffalo meat is drier and a bit gamier than beef — Tim says it's what fresh beef should taste like.

PATTIES

1 1/2 lb	750 g	ground bison*
3	3	cloves garlic, finely chopped
1	1	medium jalapeño, finely chopped
1	1	egg
1/2 cup	125 mL	chopped onion
		pepper to taste
		olive oil (as needed)
		salt to taste
		Tabasco sauce (as desired)

*You can substitute ground beef.

In a bowl, mix together all the meat patty ingredients. Shape into patties about 1/2 inch (1.25 cm) thick. Place grill about 4 inches (10 cm) from coals and brush with olive oil. Brush patties with olive oil. Grill over low heat, turning once, 4 to 5 minutes per side, until patties reach desired doneness. Season with salt. Serve with Tabasco sauce.

BUILDING BLOCKS

The predominant building block is spiciness from the Tabasco sauce. An off-dry rosé with some sweetness offsets the spiciness.

FLAVORS

Choose an off-dry rosé with earthy flavor to work with the earthy flavor of onion and garlic.

The predominant building block is spiciness from the horseradish. An off-dry rosé with some sweetness offsets the spiciness.

FLAVORS

Choose an off-dry rosé with some mineral and spicy flavors to draw out the flavors of the scallions and horseradish.

Scallion and Roast Beef Rolls

SERVES 4

When serving a variety of appetizers for a dinner party, choose a few that can be made in a flash. This appetizer definitely falls into the category of quick, easy and inexpensive.

1 cup	250 mL	cream cheese
2 Tbsp	25 mL	horseradish (or as desired)
1 tsp	5 mL	dried mustard
		salt and pepper to taste
12	12	thin slices deli roast beef
12	12	scallions, washed and trimmed

In a bowl, combine cream cheese, horseradish, dried mustard, salt and pepper. Thinly spread on one half of a slice of beef. Lay an onion on the mixture at one end. Tightly roll up beef. Repeat for remaining slices. Refrigerate until ready to serve.

BUILDING BLOCKS

The predominant building blocks are sweetness from the brown sugar and spiciness from the black pepper and cayenne. An off-dry rosé with some sweetness works with the brown sugar and offsets the spiciness.

FLAVORS

Choose an off-dry rosé with candy apple flavor to match the caramelized flavor of brown sugar.

Sweet and Spicy Rubbed Pork

SERVES 4

The flavors of this simple rub are a natural complement to pork.

SWEET AND SPICY RUB

¼ cup	50 mL	each brown sugar and salt
1 Tbsp	15 mL	black pepper
½ tsp	2 mL	cayenne (or as desired)
4	4	pork chops

Preheat oven to 350°F (180°C). In a medium bowl, mix together the rub ingredients. Sprinkle on chops. Wrap with plastic wrap and refrigerate 3 to 4 hours. In a skillet, grill chops over medium heat for 12 to 15 minutes, until almost done. Coat thickly with rub and finish cooking in the oven for about 7 minutes, until rub is caramelized. Discard leftover rub.

Chicken and Andouille Jambalaya

SERVES 4

The Choctaw Indians of Louisiana were the first to use dried, ground sassafras leaves as a seasoning. We now call this seasoning filé or gumbo filé when used in Creole and Cajun cooking.

SEASONING MIX

2	2	bay leaves
1 Tbsp	15 mL	dried parsley
1 tsp	5 mL	each salt, gumbo filé powder*, dried thyme, garlic powder
1/2 tsp	2 mL	each ground black pepper, dried mustard, chili powder, ground cumin
1/2 tsp	2 mL	cayenne (or as desired)
1/4 tsp	1 mL	ground cloves
3 Tbsp	45 mL	butter
2 cups	500 mL	chopped onion
1 cup	250 mL	each chopped green bell pepper and celery
1 lb	500 g	lean pork, cut into 1/2-inch (1.25-cm) cubes
1 cup	250 mL	shredded cooked ham
6	6	smoked Andouille sausages, sliced 1/2 inch (1.25 cm) thick
1 1/2 cups	375 mL	raw long-grain white rice
3 cups	750 mL	chicken stock
2 cups	500 mL	diced tomatoes

*Gumbo filé powder is used as a thickening agent and has little flavor. If you can't find any, use a mixture of about 2 Tbsp (25 mL) flour and 1/4 cup (50 mL) water.

Combine all the seasoning mix ingredients and set aside. In a heavy pot, melt butter over low heat. Add onion, green pepper, celery, pork and ham. Cook for 10 minutes, stirring constantly. Stir in sausage and add seasoning mix. Cook another 20 minutes. Add rice, increase heat to medium and cook 5 minutes, stirring and scraping sides and bottom of pot, until rice is lightly browned. Add stock and tomatoes. Increase heat to high; bring to a boil and cook, uncovered, 5 minutes. Cover pot, reduce heat to low and cook another 40 minutes, stirring gently every 10 minutes. If too dry, add more stock. Serve hot.

BUILDING BLOCKS

The predominant building block is spiciness from the chili powder. An off-dry rosé with some sweetness offsets the spiciness.

FLAVORS

Choose an off-dry rosé with some mineral and spicy tones to match the spice flavors in the seasoning.

JAMBALAYA AND WINE

When pairing wine with jambalaya, consider the spiciness first. If you prefer a very hot and spicy version, choose a white wine with some sweetness. The sweetness will offset the spiciness and cool your palate between bites. Rosés with a hint of sweetness work as well.

If you prefer a milder jamabalaya, choose wine according to the flesh used, such as shrimp, chicken, ham or duck. Recipes using shellfish require a crisp, dry white wine. Chicken versions go nicely with a well-balanced, medium-bodied, smooth white. Ham jambalaya is great with an off-dry white. Duck, because it's greasy, demands an austere red with fattiness.

BUILDING BLOCKS

The predominant building blocks are sweetness from the palm sugar and spiciness from the chili. An off-dry rosé with some sweetness works with the palm sugar and offsets the spiciness.

FLAVORS

Choose an off-dry rosé with pineapple and tropical flavors to work with the flavors in the Thai seasoning and match the flavor of papaya.

SHREDDING PAPAYA

While shredded green papaya is available at most Asian markets, freshly shredded green papaya has a delicious, sweet floral sap. To shred papaya, peel the fruit whole. Holding the flesh in one hand, use a meat cleaver in the other to carefully make deep cuts, very close together, all around the flesh. Use a paring knife to cut the flesh from top to bottom, creating long shreds.

Classic Dried Shrimp and Green Papaya Salad

SERVES 4

This classic Thai salad serves as a great replacement for mixed greens to accompany barbecued chicken or fish in the summer.

DRIED SHRIMP MIXTURE

4	4	cloves garlic, minced
1	1	green Thai chili, chopped*
¼ cup	50 mL	peanuts
3 Tbsp	45 mL	dried shrimp*
2	2	green beans

DRESSING

2 Tbsp	25 mL	each fresh lime juice and fish sauce*
2 tsp	10 mL	palm sugar*
2	2	small tomatoes, chopped
2	2	medium carrots, shredded
2 cups	500 mL	shredded peeled green papaya*

*Thai chili, dried shrimp, fish sauce, palm sugar and shredded green papaya are available at Asian supermarkets. For best results, shred fresh papaya yourself. See sidebar for instructions.

In a mortar and pestle, grind garlic and chili to a paste. Add peanuts and dried shrimp and grind into small pieces. Slice green beans into ³/₄-inch (2-cm) pieces, add to mortar and grind. To make dressing, in a small bowl, combine all dressing ingredients. Set aside. In a bowl, combine dried shrimp mixture, tomatoes, carrots and papaya. Divide mixture among plates. Top with dressing.

Mediterranean Crab Cakes with Chipotle Mayonnaise

SERVES 4

These crab cakes can also be served with the Lime Dipping Sauce on page 99.

CRAB CAKES

1/2 lb	250 g	fresh shelled crabmeat, drained*
3	3	green onions, finely chopped
1 cup	250 mL	soft bread crumbs
1/4 cup	50 mL	finely chopped fresh cilantro
1/2 tsp	2 mL	diced Thai green chili
3 Tbsp	45 mL	mayonnaise
1/2 lb	250 g	small shrimp, peeled and deveined
		salt and white pepper to taste

CHIPOTLE MAYONNAISE

1/2 cup	125 mL	mayonnaise
3 Tbsp	45 mL	chipotle sauce (see sidebar)

*If you can't find fresh crabmeat (out of the shell), substitute with fake crab.

Preheat oven to 350°F (180°C). In a large bowl, mix together all crab cake ingredients. Divide mixture into 4 balls. Press into patties about 2 inches (5 cm) across and $^1/_2$ inch (1.25 cm) thick. Cover and chill for one hour.

In a non-stick skillet, brown patties over medium heat on both sides. Transfer to a non-stick baking sheet and bake 10 minutes, until heated through and crisp on both sides. In a bowl, combine mayonnaise and chipotle sauce. Serve crab cakes hot with chipotle mayonnaise.

BUILDING BLOCKS

The predominant building block is spiciness from the green chili and chipotle sauce. An off-dry rosé with some sweetness offsets the spiciness.

FLAVORS

Choose an off-dry rosé with some herbal and grassy notes to draw out the subtle flavor of cilantro.

CHIPOTLE SAUCE

4	4	jalapeño chilies*
3	3	ancho chilies*
5	5	cloves garlic, skin on
1	1	small onion, diced
2 cups	500 mL	water
1/2 tsp	2 mL	salt
1 Tbsp	15 mL	cumin seed
1 tsp	5 mL	honey (if necessary)

*Chilies are sometimes difficult to find. Your local supermarket manager can order them for you.

Remove seeds and stems from chilies. In a dry skillet, cook chilies over medium heat until just smoking, about 2 minutes per side. Remove from heat. Meanwhile, place garlic cloves in toaster oven on broil. Roast until soft and aromatic, 5 to 6 minutes. Let cool and peel.

Return the skillet to low heat and add garlic, onion, water and salt. Simmer until chilies are soft, about 30 minutes. Meanwhile, place cumin seeds in dry skillet and toast, about 2 minutes. Grind in a coffee grinder until powdery.

Transfer cumin, chilies, garlic and onion to a food processor or blender. Add a little simmering water and purée until thick, but not stiff. Add more water if needed. If sauce tastes bitter, add honey. Let cool. Refrigerate until needed. The sauce will last up to 10 days in the refrigerator and up to 4 months in the freezer.

Rare Roasted Wild Tuna with Amazing Berry-Butter Sauce

SERVES 4

Thanks to all the butter, this sauce is very rich. Only a little is needed to accompany each tuna fillet. Any leftover sauce can be served with steak along with a red wine with forward berry character and soft tannin and soft acidity.

BERRY-BUTTER SAUCE

½ lb	250 g	cold butter, cubed
¼ cup	50 mL	minced shallots or green onions
1 cup	250 mL	each rosé and fish stock
2 Tbsp	25 mL	minced fresh ginger
		salt and pepper to taste
2 cups	500 mL	fresh berries (of choice)
2 Tbsp	25 mL	dark maple syrup
4	4	wild tuna fillets
		mixed greens

Preheat oven to 375°F (190°C). In a large sauté pan, melt 2 Tbsp (25 mL) butter over medium heat. Cook shallots 2 to 5 minutes, until tender. Stir in wine, stock, ginger, salt and pepper. Add berries and maple syrup. Cook, stirring, over high heat for 10 to 15 minutes, until reduced to one-quarter and almost syrupy. Gradually whisk in remaining butter, 1 cube at a time, until blended. Keep warm.

Meanwhile, sear tuna over high heat on barbecue or grill until browned on all sides. Bake 3 to 4 minutes, until tuna flakes easily with fork. Place fillets on mixed greens. Top with berry-butter sauce and serve.

Texas Dry Rub Chicken Wings

SERVES 4

The secret to a delicious dry rub is using equal portions of salt and sugar. Salt draws the juices to the surface, while sugar soaks them up and glazes the flesh.

2 lb	1 kg	chicken wings, trimmed

DRY RUB

1/4 cup	50 mL	each salt and sugar
2 Tbsp	25 mL	chili powder
1 Tbsp	15 mL	each black pepper, celery salt, dried mustard, garlic powder, onion powder
1/2 tsp	2 mL	dried lemon peel (optional)
pinch	pinch	cayenne pepper

Preheat oven to 350°F (180°C). In a large pot of boiling, salted water, parboil wings for 15 minutes. Meanwhile, in a bowl combine dry rub ingredients. Toss wings in rub. Place on a baking sheet sprayed with non-stick cooking spray and bake 20 to 25 minutes, until crispy.

Chicken Satay in Peking Sauce

SERVES 4

Peking sauce is another term for hoisin sauce, used as a flavoring agent in Chinese cuisine. It is a reddish-brown, sweet and spicy sauce with flavors of garlic, soy and chilies.

3	3	large cloves garlic, thinly sliced
1/4 cup	50 mL	fresh lime juice
1 Tbsp	15 mL	finely grated fresh ginger
		salt and pepper to taste
3	3	boneless, skinless chicken breasts, cubed
		lime wedges (for garnish)
1/2 cup	125 mL	Peking or hoisin sauce*

*Peking or hoisin sauce is available at Asian supermarkets and most Western supermarkets.

In a shallow glass dish, combine garlic, lime juice and ginger. Season with salt and pepper. Add chicken cubes to marinade. Cover and refrigerate for 1 hour. Thread chicken on pre-soaked wooden skewers. Grill until chicken is cooked through, about 15 minutes. Garnish with lime wedges and serve hot with Peking sauce.

FLAVORS

Choose an off-dry rosé with berry and spicy flavors to complement the flavors of chili powder, pepper and cayenne.

CHICKEN WINGS AND WINE

An off-dry rosé is the best wine style for chicken wings. It offers soft acidity that cuts through the greasiness of the skin on chicken wings and a hint of sweetness that pairs well with most wing sauces, such as honey garlic, barbecue, sweet and sour or mango spice. With suicide sauces or any hot and spicy versions made from hot peppers, the sweetness and sourness (acidity) in an off-dry rosé subdue the heat on one's palate.

BUILDING BLOCKS

The predominant building block is sweetness from the Peking sauce. An off-dry rosé with some sweetness matches the Peking sauce.

FLAVORS

Choose an off-dry rosé with light cherry flavor to work with the flavors of chicken and Peking sauce.

BUILDING BLOCKS

The predominant building block is spiciness from the cumin seeds, black pepper and chipotle sauce. An off-dry rosé with some sweetness offsets the spiciness.

FLAVORS

Choose an off-dry rosé with lots of berry flavor to work with the smoky flavor of the mayonnaise and toasty flavor of the cumin crust.

Cumin-Polenta Crusted Pork Loin with Chipotle Mayonnaise

SERVES 4

Homemade chipotle sauce adds an incredible roasted flavor to the mayonnaise that works well with pork.

4	4	pork loins
1/4 cup	50 mL	cornmeal
1 Tbsp	15 mL	cumin seeds
1/2 tsp	2 mL	each salt and black pepper
2 Tbsp	25 mL	olive oil

CHIPOTLE MAYONNAISE

1/2 cup	125 mL	mayonnaise
2 to 3 Tbsp	25 to 45 mL	chipotle sauce (see page 121)

Preheat oven to 350°F (180°C). Dry pork loins. In a bowl, combine cornmeal, cumin seeds, salt and pepper. Transfer mixture to a plate. Roll pork loins in cornmeal mixture, coating completely, including sides. In a large skillet, heat oil over medium heat. Transfer pork loins to skillet. Sear until golden, about 2 minutes per side. Transfer loins to a non-stick baking sheet. Roast until meat is white, 45 minutes to 1 hour. In a bowl, combine mayonnaise and chipotle sauce. Place pork loins on plates with chipotle mayonnaise. Slice and serve.

Hazel's Meatballs

SERVES 4

My mom's good friend Hazel Legge created this recipe. The meatballs taste great both sweet or sweet and spicy and can be frozen for up to 2 months. Thanks, Hazel!

MEATBALLS

2 lb	1 kg	lean ground beef
15	15	soda crackers, crushed
1	1	onion, minced
1	1	egg, beaten
1 Tbsp	15 mL	barbecue sauce
		salt and pepper to taste

SAUCE

1 1/3 cups	**325 mL**	barbecue sauce
1 cup	**250 mL**	cranberry sauce
		chili paste (as desired)

Preheat oven to 400°F (200°C). In a bowl, mix together meatball ingredients. Roll into meatballs. Place meatballs on a baking sheet sprayed with non-stick cooking spray. Bake 20 to 25 minutes. Transfer to a roasting pan. Fold sauce ingredients into meatballs. Reduce heat to 350°F (180°C). Bake meatballs, uncovered, 1 hour. Place on serving dish and insert a toothpick into each.

Hot Coconut Chicken Soup

SERVES 4

The coconut milk makes this soup hardy enough to be served on its own as a meal — accompanied by a glass of chilled rosé, of course.

1	1	cooked chicken (2 lb/1 kg)
1	1	piece galangal*
4 cups	**1 L**	cups coconut milk
1 Tbsp	**15 mL**	vegetable oil
2	2	stalks lemon grass, bruised with mortar and pestle and cut into 1-inch (2.5-cm) lengths*
2 cups	**500 mL**	coconut cream
2 Tbsp	**25 mL**	fresh lime juice
1 Tbsp	**15 mL**	fish sauce*
1/2 tsp	**2 mL**	chili paste* (or as desired)
1	1	green onion, chopped (for garnish)

*Galangal, lemon grass, fish sauce and chili paste are available at Asian supermarkets.

Cut chicken into bite-sized pieces. Wash the galangal root and cut into thin rounds. In a saucepan, heat oil over high heat, then add coconut milk and bring to a boil. Add chicken, galangal root and lemon grass. Reduce heat to medium. Add coconut cream, lime juice, fish sauce and chili paste. Simmer for 15 minutes. Adjust seasoning, adding more lime juice for sourness and more chili paste for heat if desired. Serve hot, garnished with green onion.

BUILDING BLOCKS

The predominant building blocks are fruitiness and sweetness from the cranberry sauce and spiciness from the chili paste. An off-dry rosé with some sweetness works with cranberry sauce and offsets the spiciness.

FLAVORS

Choose an off-dry rosé with cranberry flavor to match the flavor of cranberries in the sauce.

BUILDING BLOCKS

The predominant building blocks are fruitiness and sweetness from the coconut and spiciness from the chili paste. An off-dry rosé with some sweetness works with the coconut and offsets the spiciness.

FLAVORS

Choose an off-dry rosé with apple or pineapple flavors to work with the flavor of coconut.

GALANGAL

A cousin to ginger, galangal root is pale yellow with pinkish sprouts and is a well-used ingredient in Indonesian and other Southeast Asian cuisine, especially Thai cuisine. Its flavor resembles lemon-ginger, but it's more pronounced than ginger. It partners well with lemon grass and garlic. Galangal can be purchased fresh or dried. If using dried, add the soaking liquid to the dish you are creating for more flavor.

Caramelized Onion, Chèvre and Walnut Pizza

SERVES 4

While some people add sugar to their onions, I believe the natural, concentrated sugars from the caramelized onions are sweet enough.

½ cup	125 mL	finely chopped toasted walnuts
¼ cup	50 mL	olive oil
4	4	cloves garlic, minced
6	6	large onions, minced
		salt and pepper to taste
2	2	pizza crusts, parcooked (see sidebar)
2 cups	500 mL	crumbled chèvre

Preheat oven to 350°F (180°C). Sprinkle walnuts onto a baking sheet and bake until toasted, about 5 minutes. Watch carefully to avoid burning. Remove from sheet and set aside. Set a pizza stone in oven.

In a large skillet, heat oil over medium heat. Add garlic and sauté until aromatic. Add onions. Season with salt and pepper. Reduce heat to low. Cover pan and sauté for 25 to 30 minutes, until onions are caramel brown. Watch closely. Add a touch more oil if needed. Fold in walnuts and coat with onions. Remove mixture from pan. Let cool.

Spread onion-walnut mixture on pizza crusts. Sprinkle with crumbled chèvre. Remove pizza stone from oven. Set a pizza on stone and bake for 10 to 12 minutes, until crust is golden and cheese has melted. Bake second pizza. Serve hot.

SIMPLE PIZZA DOUGH

MAKES 2 PIZZAS

1	1	envelope dry yeast
1 cup	250 mL	warm water
3 cups	750 mL	flour
1 tsp	5 mL	salt

Sprinkle yeast over the water in a food processor. Pulse once or twice to mix. Let sit until mixture foams. Add 1 cup (250 mL) flour and process until smooth. Add most of the remaining flour and all the salt. Process again until mixture forms a ball. Test with your finger — if dough feels sticky, add remaining flour.

Knead lightly on a floured surface. Place in an oiled bowl, turning to coat the surface. Cover bowl with a damp cloth and let dough rise at room temperature until doubled in bulk. Preheat oven to 450°F (230°C). Punch the dough down and knead lightly. Divide dough into 2 portions. Use immediately or freeze until needed.

Garlicky Barbecue Baby Back Ribs

SERVES 4

I first experienced this rib sauce years ago at a rib festival. Over the years, I've modified the recipe, finally coming up with this delicious rendition.

SAUCE

2	2	large onions, minced
1	1	bulb garlic, cloves peeled and minced
1 ⅓ cups	325 mL	ketchup
¼ cup	50 mL	balsamic vinegar
pinch	pinch	cayenne (or as desired)
6 to 8 cups	1½ to 2 L	root beer
2	2	racks baby back ribs*

*Have the butcher remove the membrane off the back of the ribs.

In a pot, combine all the sauce ingredients and simmer over low heat until thick and chunky, about 45 minutes. Meanwhile, in a large pot, bring root beer to a boil over high heat. Reduce heat to medium. Parboil ribs in root beer for 30 minutes or until the liquid turns clear. Baste ribs in sauce. Barbecue on hot grill until sauce has caramelized, about 5 minutes per side. Baste ribs again. Serve hot with leftover sauce.

BUILDING BLOCKS

The predominant building block is spiciness from the cayenne. An off-dry rosé with some sweetness offsets the spiciness.

FLAVORS

Choose an off-dry rosé with earthy flavor to match the earthy flavor of onion and garlic.

13

LIGHT, **FRUITY** REDS

PREDOMINANT BUILDING BLOCKS

- *Sourness and fruitiness, sometimes with some bitterness*

FLAVORS

- *Cherry, strawberry and gooseberry; sometimes spicy and mineral-like flavors*

Gamays, dry rosés and certain varietals, such as pinot noir, fall into the light, fruity red style. Served slightly chilled, they're great summer wines.

The factors that determine wines that fall into this style are the grape variety, the geography, climate and soil conditions of the wine region, and the winemaking techniques employed. During fermentation the must (juice) spends a short or long time with the pomace (skins, seeds and stalks), depending on the ripeness of the harvest, the grape variety being vinified and the style of wine to be made. The longer the wine spends on the pomace during fermentation, the deeper the color and higher the tannin. To produce light, fruity reds, the must usually spends a short time on the pomace. Some are aged in oak for a short time, but even with aging, the wines retain fresh acidity and fruitiness.

Gamay also undergoes a process called carbonic maceration, which occurs over three to seven days. Whole grapes are put into a vat with carbon dioxide. The weight of the grapes crushes the lower ones and causes them to expel juice. Two fermentations then begin, one within the juice and the other as an intracellular fermentation inside the whole grapes. This kind of fermentation creates ethanol as well as various appealing aroma components. After a few weeks, the wine is continued as usual. Gamay Beaujolais, from France, is a famous gamay wine, and there are four different versions — Beaujolais, Beaujolais-Villages, Beaujolais Supérieur and Beaujolais Crus.

The regions in the sidebar are stylistically noted for producing light, fruity red wines.

REGIONS

GAMAY
Canada (British Columbia, Ontario)
France (Beaujolais, Languedoc)

DRY ROSÉ
Canada (British Columbia, Ontario)
Chile
France (Languedoc, Provence, Southern Côtes du Rhone, Tavel, Southern Rhone)
Greece
Italy (Bardolino)
Spain (Catalonia, Navarra)

PINOT NOIR
Canada (British Columbia, Ontario)
France (Burgundy)
United States (California, Oregon, Washington State)

HARMONY CHART

Pinot Noir

FOOD AFFINITIES

SEAFOOD	MEAT POULTRY	HERBS SPICES	SAUCES	CHEESE NUTS	VEGETABLES FRUITS PASTAS GRAINS
Salmon	Bacon	Basil	Butter	Brie	Beets
Tuna	Beef	Bay leaf	Mustard	Feta	Black-eyed peas
	Duck	Black pepper	Red wine	Goat's-milk brie	Cabbage (red)
	Game hen	Clove	Soy	Jack	Celery root
	Quail	Galangal	Tomato	Taleggio	Jasmine rice
	Squab	Garlic		Walnuts	Kalamata olives
		Lavender			Kale
		Thyme			Mushrooms (all varieties)
		Turmeric			Mustard greens
					Pasta (whole wheat)
					Pomegranates
					Red peppers

FOOD CHALLENGES

SEAFOOD	MEAT POULTRY	HERBS SPICES	SAUCES	CHEESE NUTS	VEGETABLES FRUITS PASTAS GRAINS
Oysters (raw)	None	Cilantro	Citrus	Blue	Artichokes
Smoked fish		Cumin	Cream	Cheddar (aged)	Asparagus
Sushi		Curry	Vinaigrette	Gouda (aged)	Green beans

BEST METHODS OF PREPARATION
Braising, grilling, roasting, sautéing

COMPLEMENTARY CUISINES
French Contemporary, Mediterranean,
Northern Californian, Northern Italian

BEST SEASONS
Spring, summer, fall

IDEAL OCCASIONS
Barbecue, evening grilling, picnic

Chilled Sour Cherry Soup with Sour Cream and Thyme

SERVES 4

This is a refreshing soup for picnics and hot summer evenings.

2 tsp	10 mL	butter
1 Tbsp	15 mL	minced shallots
1 lb	500 g	sour cherries, pitted
1 cup	250 mL	chicken stock
2 Tbsp	25 mL	each fresh lemon juice and fresh thyme
½ cup	125 mL	sour cream

In a skillet, melt butter over low heat and sauté shallots until soft. Add cherries and stock. Increase heat to medium and simmer for 15 minutes. In a food processor or blender, purée the mixture. Strain soup. Add lemon juice and thyme. Chill for 2 hours. Just before serving, blend in sour cream.

BUILDING BLOCKS

The predominant building blocks are sourness and fruitiness from the lemon juice, sour cherries and sour cream. A light, fruity red with sourness and fruitiness is a match.

FLAVORS

Choose a light, fruity red with cherry flavor to match the cherry flavor of the soup.

FRESH CHERRIES

While you can use frozen, pitted cherries for this recipe, fresh cherries produce a more flavorful soup that works more appropriately with a light, fruity red wine. Store cherries unwashed in the refrigerator and wash only before using. Let warm to room temperature before working with them. Hand-held cherry pitters are available at kitchen shops and are quite inexpensive. Be careful when pitting cherries — their juice stains clothing.

BUILDING BLOCKS

The predominant building block is saltiness from the tamarind and fish sauce and fruitiness from the green mango. A light, fruity red with sourness and fruitiness offsets the saltiness and works with the green mango.

FLAVORS

Choose a light, fruity red with pineapple flavor to match the mango flavor.

BUYING AND CLEANING TROUT

When buying fresh trout, look for firm flesh and a clean smell. Once home, wash the fish under cool water, pat dry and cover in plastic wrap. Store in the coldest part of the refrigerator. While trout will last up to 2 days, using it immediately ensures the freshest taste.

Spicy, Crispy Trout Soup with Green Mango

SERVES 4

When deep-frying the trout, make sure the oil is hot, almost smoking. If the temperature is too low, the fish will soak up too much oil.

SOUP

6 cups	1.5 L	chicken stock
4	4	stalks lemon grass, bruised in mortar and pestle and cut into 1-inch (2.5-cm) lengths*
4	4	shallots, sliced
4	4	kaffir lime leaves*
1/4 cup	50 mL	each green mango, shredded, and tamarind purée*
1/2 cup	125 mL	fish sauce*

TROUT

1 lb	500 g	rainbow trout fillets
1/4 cup	50 mL	milk
		flour seasoned with salt and pepper (for dredging)
		vegetable oil (for deep-frying)
2 Tbsp	25 mL	each finely chopped green onion and fresh cilantro

*Lemon grass, kaffir lime leaves, tamarind purée and fish sauce are available at Asian supermarkets.

In a saucepan, bring stock to a boil over high heat. Add remaining soup ingredients. Lower heat and simmer for about 30 minutes, until flavors are well combined. Keep hot.

Meanwhile, cut fish into bite-sized lengths and pat dry. Pour milk into a bowl. Place seasoned flour in a dish. Coat fish in milk and, without drying, dredge in flour. In a large skillet, heat oil over high heat, until almost smoking. Deep-fry fish until golden and crispy, 6 to 7 minutes. Drain on paper towel. Add green onion and coriander to soup. Serve immediately. Add trout to soup as you eat.

Radicchio and Arugula Salad with Fresh Thyme

SERVES 4

Radicchio and arugula are popular Italian vegetables used in salads, pastas and risottos. In true Italian style, this salad is simple and uses fresh ingredients and herbs.

¼ cup	50 mL	olive oil
2 to 3 Tbsp	25 to 45 mL	red wine vinegar
pinch	pinch	salt
½ tsp	2 mL	freshly ground black pepper
3 cups	750 mL	radicchio, torn into bite-size pieces
3 cups	750 mL	arugula, tough stems removed and leaves torn into bite-size pieces
2 Tbsp	25 mL	finely chopped fresh thyme

In a small bowl, combine oil and vinegar. Balance to taste. Add salt and pepper. In a large bowl, toss together lettuces and thyme. Pour vinaigrette over salad, toss and serve.

BUILDING BLOCKS

The predominant building blocks are sourness from the red wine vinegar and a hint of bitterness from the radicchio. A light, fruity red with sourness and fruitiness and a hint of bitterness is a match.

FLAVORS

Choose a light, fruity red with a peppery finish to work with the black pepper.

The predominant building blocks are sourness from the feta and fruitiness from the beets. A light, fruity red with sourness and fruitiness is a match.

FLAVORS

Choose a light, fruity red with earthy flavor to match the fruity and earthy flavors of roasted beets.

Roasted Beets with Feta

SERVES 4

Roasting concentrates the fruitiness in beets, making them an ideal partner for red wine.

DRESSING

2	2	cloves garlic, minced
1/2 cup	125 mL	each olive oil and red wine
2 Tbsp	25 mL	finely chopped fresh thyme
		salt and pepper to taste
7	7	medium beets
1 cup	250 mL	water
3/4 cup	175 mL	crumbled feta cheese

Preheat oven to 375°F (190°C). In a bowl, combine the dressing ingredients. Cover and refrigerate until needed. Arrange beets in a roasting pan and add water. Cover and bake 15 minutes or until tender. Peel beets, then cut into cubes and place in a large bowl. Cover and refrigerate for about 2 hours. Just before serving, toss beets with dressing and feta.

Baked Fennel and Parmesan with Risotto

SERVES 4

This Italian-style vegetarian dish is ideal for summer dining or can be served alongside grilled chicken.

3	**3**	heads fennel
2	**2**	cloves garlic, thinly sliced
½ cup	**125 mL**	julienned red pepper
2 Tbsp	**25 mL**	olive oil
		salt and pepper to taste
½ cup	**125 mL**	freshly grated Parmesan cheese

RISOTTO

2 ½ cups	**625 mL**	vegetable stock
½ cup	**125 mL**	olive oil
½	**½**	small onion, finely chopped
2	**2**	cloves garlic, minced
1 cup	**250 mL**	arborio rice

Preheat oven to 350°F (180°C). Cut tops off fennel and slice bulbs into 4 wedges. In a large pot of boiling, salted water, boil fennel for about 5 minutes, until wilted. Remove from water and cool under cold water. Drain on paper towel. In a bowl, toss together fennel, garlic, pepper, oil, salt and pepper, then arrange in baking dish. Sprinkle with Parmesan. Bake until cheese is golden, 15 to 20 minutes. Keep warm.

Meanwhile, to make risotto, in a pot, bring stock to a boil. In a large, heavy pot, heat oil over medium heat. Add onion. Stir in garlic and rice, coating rice with oil. Make sure rice is very hot. Slowly add about ¼ cup (50 mL) stock, stirring constantly until stock is absorbed. Continue adding stock until rice is firm to bite and risotto is creamy, 15 to 20 minutes. Stir in one more ladle of stock before transferring risotto to plates, topped with baked fennel.

BUILDING BLOCKS

The predominant building blocks are saltiness from the Parmesan and a hint of bitterness from the fennel. A light, fruity red with sourness and fruitiness and a hint of bitterness offsets the saltiness and works with the fennel.

FLAVORS

Choose a light, fruity red with some tannin and earthy flavor to work with the fennel and match the flavor of Parmesan.

BUILDING BLOCKS

The predominant building block is sourness from the chèvre. A light, fruity red with sourness is a match.

FLAVORS

Choose a light, fruity red with some earthy flavor to bring out the earthiness in the whole-wheat crust.

Whole-Wheat Tortilla Pizza with Rosemary and Thyme Chèvre

SERVES 4

When I'm not in the mood to cook a big meal or test new dishes, I make crispy pizzas using tortilla shells. This is one of the fastest to make and can be wedged and served as an appetizer or as a meal along with a side salad.

2	2	cloves garlic, minced
3/4 cup	175 mL	crumbled fresh chèvre
2 Tbsp	25 mL	each finely chopped fresh rosemary and fresh thyme
2 tsp	10 mL	olive oil
		salt and pepper to taste
4	4	whole-wheat flour tortillas, 6-inch (15-cm) diameter

Preheat oven to 300°F (150°C). In a small bowl, combine all ingredients except for tortillas. Place tortillas on oven rack and toast until crisp, about 2 minutes. Spread chèvre mixture onto warm tortillas and serve immediately.

Puffed Pork Rolls with Feta Salsa

SERVES 4

Thomas Dietzel is one of my favorite Canadian chefs. This is an easy but interesting recipe he shared with me more than a decade ago.

STUFFING

¼ lb	125 g	spinach, blanched
1	1	small egg, lightly beaten
¼ lb	125 g	each Saint Paulin cheese, shredded, and ground lean pork
¼ tsp	1 mL	salt
Pinch	Pinch	pepper

PORK ROLLS

4	4	lean pork schnitzels
4	4	prepared puff pastry squares
		egg wash (1 egg yolk beaten with 1 tsp/5 mL water)

FETA SALSA

3 Tbsp	45 mL	each diced onion and tequila
1 Tbsp	15 mL	tomato paste
½ cup	125 mL	diced tomatoes
3 oz	85 g	feta cheese, crumbled
		salt and pepper to taste

To make stuffing, squeeze out excess water from spinach. Chop coarsely. In a large mixing bowl, mix all stuffing ingredients. Set aside.

Preheat oven to 350°F (180°C). To make pork rolls, using a mallet, pound pork schnitzels until very thin. Spread each schnitzel with a quarter of the stuffing. Roll up tightly, tucking in ends. On a lightly floured work surface, roll out puff pastry squares until same length as pork rolls. Wrap pastry around each roll. Brush end of pastry with egg wash to seal. Place rolls on a baking sheet sprayed with non-stick cooking spray. Bake 20 to 25 minutes, until meat is cooked and pastry is golden.

To make salsa, in a small saucepan, simmer onion, tequila and tomato paste over medium heat for 1 minute. Stir in remaining ingredients. Simmer for 15 minutes.

Place pork rolls on plates and slice each into 4 slices. Top with a generous spoonful of salsa.

BUILDING BLOCKS

The predominant building blocks are sourness and fruitiness from the tomatoes and feta and a hint of bitterness from the spinach. A light, fruity red with sourness and fruitiness and a hint of bitterness is a match.

FLAVORS

Choose a light, fruity red with some herbal flavor to bring out the flavor of spinach.

CHAPTER 14

REDS WITH **FORWARD** FRUIT CHARACTER

PREDOMINANT BUILDING BLOCKS

- *Fruitiness and fattiness with subtle sourness and bitterness*

FLAVORS

- *Raspberry, black cherry, plum, mineral, floral, grassy and spicy*

Red wines with forward fruit are often described as concentrated, extracted, reasonably oaky with lots of slightly sweet (sometimes over-ripe) fruit, soft acidity and soft tannin. While fruitiness takes center stage as this wine style's predominant building block, alcohol levels can be as high as 14 percent, adding an oily mouthfeel and creamy texture to the wines. Many New World regions — California in particular — are noted for producing red wines with forward fruit character, such as Merlot and Zinfandel.

The factors that determine wines that fall into this style are the grape variety, the geography, climate and soil conditions of the wine region, and the winemaking techniques employed. While able to grow in various climates, red grapes gain more richness, weight and fruitiness when grown in hotter conditions. The soft tannin and soft acidity in these wines is developed through various winemaking techniques. For example, the juice may be fermented on the skins for fewer days. The juice may also be fermented with only the skins and pulp, not the stems, which imparts too much bitterness — an undesirable quality in reds with forward fruit character. As well, once fermented, the wine undergoes a malolactic fermentation, transforming some of the wine's tart malic acid or sourness into softer lactic acid.

The regions above right are stylistically noted for producing red wines with forward fruit character.

REGIONS

MERLOT
Australia
Canada (British Columbia, Ontario)
Chile
New Zealand
United States (California)

OTHERS
Burgundy – France
Côtes du Rhone-Villages – France
Grenache – Australia
Malbec – France
Shiraz – Australia
Zinfandel – United States (California)

HARMONY CHART

Zinfandel

FOOD AFFINITIES

SEAFOOD	MEAT POULTRY	HERBS SPICES	SAUCES	CHEESE NUTS	VEGETABLES FRUITS PASTAS GRAINS
Crab	Bacon	Basil	Balsamic reduction	Blue	Corn
Hot-smoked salmon	Beef	Bay leaf	Barbecue	Cheddar (medium)	Eggplant
Mussels	Buffalo	Chili (mild)	Berry (little to no sweetness)	Chèvre (aged)	Polenta
Shrimp	Pork	Filé	Roasted tomato	Parmesan	Tomatoes (roasted, dried)
	Quail	Oregano	Rosé		Zucchini
	Sausage	Paprika	Salsa (mild)		

FOOD CHALLENGES

SEAFOOD	MEAT POULTRY	HERBS SPICES	SAUCES	CHEESE NUTS	VEGETABLES FRUITS PASTAS GRAINS
Oysters (raw)	Chicken (smoked)	Capers	Citrus	Gouda (aged)	Artichokes
Sardines	Pheasant	Cumin	Mayonnaise	Pecans	Asparagus
Sole	Veal	Curry	Vinaigrettes	Swiss	Green beans
Sushi		Dill			
Whitefish					

BEST METHODS OF PREPARATION
Barbecuing, braising, grilling, stews

BEST SEASONS
Summer, fall

COMPLEMENTARY CUISINES
Italian, Southwestern, Californian

IDEAL OCCASIONS
Everyday

Mozzarella and Roasted Red Pepper Bruschetta

SERVES 4

There are countless roasted red pepper recipes to work with this style of wine. The wonderful fruitiness of the roasted red pepper is mirrored in the fruit-forward character of this wine style.

1	1	large red pepper
8	8	green olives
2	2	cloves garlic, minced
½ cup	125 mL	olive oil
8	8	slices Italian bread
2	2	cloves garlic, whole
1 cup	250 mL	finely chopped fresh basil
1 lb	500 g	mozzarella cheese, thinly sliced

Cut pepper in half — don't remove seeds. Lay peppers cut sides down on a baking sheet. Under broiler, grill about 5 inches (12 cm) from heat, turning every 2 to 3 minutes to blister and char all sides, about 25 minutes total. Wrap peppers in plastic and let cool. Peel peppers, beginning at stem end. Cut off tops and discard seeds and ribs. Dice and set aside.

In a food processor or blender, blend olives, minced garlic and oil to smooth paste. Set aside. Put bread slices on baking sheet and, under broiler, grill one side until golden, about 2 minutes. Change oven's setting to 350°F (180°C). Rub toasted side with whole garlic cloves, then drizzle with olive oil paste. Top with diced peppers, then basil. Cover with mozzarella. Bake until cheese is melted and bread is toasted on the bottom and golden, about 5 minutes. Serve hot.

BUILDING BLOCKS

The predominant building block is fruitiness from the roasted red pepper. A red wine with forward fruit and some fattiness works with the roasted red pepper, while its oily mouthfeel parallels the creaminess of warm mozzarella cheese.

FLAVORS

Choose a red wine with forward fruit possessing subtle herbal notes to draw out the subtle flavor of the basil.

BUILDING BLOCKS

The predominant building block is fattiness from the olive oil, brie and butter. A red wine with forward fruit and some fattiness has an oily mouthfeel that parallels the fattiness of the oil, brie and butter.

FLAVORS

Choose a fruit-forward red with earthy flavor to work with the earthy flavors of garlic, ripened brie and mushrooms.

Ripened Brie and Rosemary Bruschetta

SERVES 4

The harmonizing flavors of garlic, ripened brie, shiitake mushrooms and rosemary are out of this world.

4	4	slices olive sourdough bread, ½ inch (1.25 cm) thick
2	2	cloves garlic
¼ cup	50 mL	olive oil
⅔ lb	350 g	ripened brie, thinly sliced
2 Tbsp	25 mL	butter
½ cup	125 mL	chopped shiitake mushrooms
1 Tbsp	15 mL	fresh rosemary, finely chopped
		salt and pepper to taste

Under broiler, grill one side of bread slices until golden, about 2 minutes. Rub toasted sides with garlic, then drizzle with olive oil. Lay brie slices on toasted sides. In a saucepan, melt butter over low heat, then lightly sauté mushrooms, about 5 minutes. Stir in remaining ingredients. Under broiler, grill bruschetta slices until cheese begins to run. Place on warm plates and top with sautéed mushrooms. Serve immediately.

BUILDING BLOCKS

The predominant building block is fattiness from the brie and pesto. A red wine with forward fruit and some fattiness has an oily mouthfeel that parallels the brie and pesto.

FLAVORS

Choose a red wine with forward fruit with some earthy flavor to work with the earthy flavor in ripened brie and nutty flavor in pesto.

Ripened Brie and Pesto en Croute

SERVES 4 TO 6

This appetizer is so flavorful and popular, I often make two of them, knowing my guests will overindulge.

1	1	loaf frozen bread dough, thawed
1	1	small ripened brie round, rind removed
½ cup	125 mL	pesto*
		egg wash (1 egg yolk beaten with 1 tsp/5 mL water)

*I often use pre-made pesto and add more fresh garlic.

Preheat oven to 375°F (190°C). Divide dough in half. On a lightly floured work surface, roll each half into a 7-inch (18-cm) circle, just larger than the brie. Place one circle on a greased baking sheet.

Cut brie in half horizontally. Spread pesto over cheese. Place other half on top and seal edges. Place brie in center of dough on the baking sheet. Brush edge of dough with water. Place remaining circle over the brie, pressing firmly on edges to seal. Brush dough with egg yolk. Place a pan of hot water in bottom of oven to create steam, which keeps the crust tender. Bake bread 25 to 30 minutes, until golden. Cool 5 minutes and cut into wedges.

Wild Mushroom and Barley Risotto

SERVES 4

This is a tasty dish for lacto-vegetarians who love wine!

2 Tbsp	25 mL	butter
½ cup	125 mL	chopped mixed wild mushrooms
		salt and pepper to taste
4 cups	1 L	vegetable stock (or as needed)
½ cup	125 mL	butter
2	2	medium cloves garlic, minced
1	1	medium onion, finely chopped
½ cup	125 mL	pearl barley, rinsed, drained
1 cup	250 mL	arborio rice
½ cup	125 mL	freshly grated Parmesan cheese
1 Tbsp	15 mL	each chopped fresh Italian parsley and fresh thyme

In a saucepan, melt butter over medium heat. Add mushrooms and a touch of water if necessary. Sauté until soft, about 5 minutes. Season with salt and pepper. Keep warm.

Meanwhile, to make risotto, in a large pot, bring stock to a boil. In a saucepan, heat butter over medium heat, add garlic and sauté until aromatic. Add onion and sauté until tender, 5 to 7 minutes. Add barley, coating with butter mixture. Slowly add about ¼ cup (50 mL) stock, stirring constantly until stock is absorbed. Add rice. Continue adding stock until barley is soft, rice is firm and risotto is creamy, 15 to 20 minutes.

Combine risotto with mushrooms, Parmesan and herbs. Stir in one more ladle of boiling broth before transferring risotto to plates. Serve hot.

CHOOSING BRIE

When choosing brie, look for one without a stabilizer. While the stabilizer gives the cheese a longer life, it doesn't allow natural ripening to occur. Brie without a stabilizer will continue to age with wonderful earthy, mushroom flavors that complement the flavors in the pesto.

BUILDING BLOCKS

The predominant building block is fattiness from the butter and cheese. A red wine with forward fruit and some fattiness has an oily mouthfeel that parallels the fat in butter and cheese.

FLAVORS

Choose an older fruit-forward red with some earthy flavor to bring out the subtle earthy flavor of wild mushrooms and Parmesan cheese.

The predominant building blocks are fruitiness from the concentrated flavor of the roasted tomatoes and subtle fattiness from the oil. A red wine with forward fruit and some fattiness works with the roasted tomatoes and has an oily mouthfeel that parallels the fat of oil.

FLAVORS

Choose a red wine with forward berry flavor to complement the fruitiness of roasted tomatoes.

Roasted Tomato Ragout with Baked Polenta

SERVES 4

Polenta is a traditional Northern Italian food made from cornmeal. It is a savory porridge that can be served hot, soft and creamy; cooled and firm; fried; grilled or baked.

ROASTED TOMATO RAGOUT

6	6	large tomatoes
2	2	medium zucchini
1	1	bulb garlic, skin on
1	1	small onion
¼ cup	50 mL	red wine
2 Tbsp	25 mL	olive oil
1 tsp	5 mL	each dried basil and dried oregano
		salt and pepper to taste
1	1	12-inch (30-cm) loaf of firm polenta, pre-made or homemade (see page 67)

Preheat oven to broil. Place tomatoes, zucchini, garlic and onion on a baking sheet sprayed with non-stick cooking spray. Broil until blackened, 7 to 10 minutes. Let cool. Peel all. Dice and place in a large pot. Add wine, oil and herbs. Season with salt and pepper. Simmer ragout over low heat for 40 to 60 minutes, until liquid is reduced to a thick stew. Keep warm.

Preheat oven to 350°F (180°C). Cut polenta into 8 rounds, each about ½ inch (1.25 cm) thick. Place on a baking sheet sprayed with non-stick cooking spray and bake until golden, 5 to 10 minutes. Place 2 rounds on each plate. Cover with ragout and serve hot.

POLENTA AND WINE

Polenta is like a blank canvas on which you can create a masterpiece of exotic, bright flavors. As a result, it can be partnered to a variety of wines, depending on two elements: the boiling liquid and the texture and flavor of the accompanying ingredients. Here are a few examples to get you started.

BOILING LIQUID	INGREDIENTS	WINE STYLE
Water	Tomatoes, zucchini, asparagus	Crisp, dry white
Water and milk	Seafood, chicken	Well-balanced, medium-bodied, smooth white
Water and milk or cream	Wild mushrooms, shallots, truffles	Big, fat white
Chicken stock	Caramelized onions, chicken	Off-dry white or off-dry rosé
Vegetable or chicken stock	Roasted tomatoes, roasted onions, roasted mushrooms, chicken	Red with forward fruit
Chicken or beef stock	Radicchio, spinach, blue cheese, Parmesan, nuts	Austere red

Tuscan Steak with Balsamic and Roasted Tomato Relish

SERVES 4

My husband loved a balsamic vinegar reduction that got too thick, so here it is.

BALSAMIC AND ROASTED TOMATO RELISH

2	2	large tomatoes
3/4 cup	175 mL	aged balsamic vinegar
1 Tbsp	15 mL	finely diced shallots
1 tsp	5 mL	each dried oregano and sugar
		salt and pepper to taste
4	4	steaks of choice

Set oven or toaster oven to broil. Place tomatoes on foil and broil for 15 to 20 minutes, until blackened. Let cool, then peel and seed. Coarsely chop tomatoes. Set aside. In a saucepan, combine remaining relish ingredients over low heat. Simmer for 25 to 30 minutes, until sauce is reduced by half. Fold in roasted tomatoes. Continue to simmer until sauce thickens to a relish, about 15 minutes. Season steaks with salt and pepper and grill to desired doneness. Serve warm relish with hot steaks.

Rack of Lamb with Mint Pesto

SERVES 4

Lamb and mint are a classic, harmonizing combination. For an Asian slant, add a touch of chili to the pesto and pair the dish with an off-dry rosé.

MINT PESTO

1/2 cup	125 mL	fresh mint leaves
1 Tbsp	15 mL	liquid honey
1 tsp	5 mL	fresh lemon juice
		salt and pepper to taste
		olive oil (as needed)
1 Tbsp	15 mL	soft butter
1	1	clove garlic, minced
4	4	racks lamb (consisting of 5 ribs), trimmed

Preheat oven to 400°F (200°C). To make pesto, in a food processor or blender, purée mint, honey, lemon juice, salt and pepper. With motor running, slowly add oil until mixture is smooth. Cover and refrigerate until needed.

In a small bowl, combine butter and garlic. Mix well. Rub mixture over lamb. Season with salt and pepper. Place lamb in a shallow roasting pan and roast to desired doneness, about 20 minutes for medium rare. Serve hot with mint pesto.

BUILDING BLOCKS

The predominant building blocks are fruitiness from the balsamic vinegar and roasted tomatoes and fattiness from the steak. A red wine with forward fruit works with the balsamic vinegar and tomatoes and has an oily mouthfeel that parallels the fat in red meat.

FLAVORS

Choose a red wine with forward berry flavor to match the fruity flavor of roasted tomato and concentrated balsamic vinegar.

BUILDING BLOCKS

The predominant building block is fattiness from the lamb, olive oil and butter. A red wine with forward fruit and some fattiness has an oily mouthfeel that parallels the fat in lamb, oil and butter.

FLAVORS

Choose any fruit-forward red with lots of berry character to work with the mint flavor in the pesto.

Manicotti with Roasted Tomato-Garlic Sauce

SERVES 4

A tasty dish for wine-loving vegetarians. Roasting the tomatoes reduces their acidity and concentrates their natural sweetness, making this dish a good match for a red with forward fruit.

SAUCE

		olive oil (as needed)
10	10	medium ripe tomatoes
1	1	bulb garlic, skin on
1	1	small onion, minced
1 Tbsp	15 mL	each finely chopped fresh oregano and fresh basil
½ cup	125 mL	red wine
10	10	manicotti shells

FILLING

2	2	eggs
½	½	red pepper, diced
1 ½ cups	375 mL	ricotta
1 cup	250 mL	shredded mozzarella
2 Tbsp	25 mL	finely chopped fresh Italian parsley
		salt and pepper to taste

Preheat oven to 450°F (230°C). Brush 2 baking sheets with oil. Place tomatoes and garlic on sheets and roast 25 to 30 minutes, until skins are charred. Let cool, then peel. In a food processor or blender, purée tomatoes, garlic and onion. Fold in oregano and basil. Pour sauce into a pan. Add wine. Simmer over low heat for 1 hour or until sauce is reduced to about 2 cups (500 mL).

Meanwhile, in a large pot of boiling, salted water, cook manicotti until al dente, 7 to 10 minutes. Dry on paper towel. Be careful not to break shells. In a large bowl, combine eggs, red pepper, ricotta, mozzarella and parsley. Season with salt and pepper. Stuff 8 shells with ricotta mixture. (The 2 extra shells get cooked in case of breakage.)

Pour about 1 cup (250 mL) sauce into a heatproof baking pan. Lay stuffed manicotti shells on top, then pour on remaining sauce. Reduce heat to 350°F (180°C). Bake, covered, about 30 minutes or until heated through. Serve hot.

Louisiana Blackened Catfish with Roasted Red Pepper Butter

SERVES 4

Normally, blackened seasoning has cayenne pepper. I've left it out here so that the dish will work with a red wine with forward fruit. If you want to add cayenne, pair the dish with a rosé offering a hint of sweetness.

BLACKENED SEASONING

3 Tbsp	45 mL	dried thyme
2 Tbsp	25 mL	each garlic powder, onion powder and paprika
1 Tbsp	15 mL	dried oregano
2 tsp	10 mL	each salt and black pepper
1 tsp	5 mL	each ground cumin and ground nutmeg

ROASTED RED PEPPER BUTTER

1	1	red pepper
1/4 cup	50 mL	soft butter
1/2 tsp	2 mL	paprika
		salt and pepper to taste

3 Tbsp	45 mL	butter
4	4	catfish fillets

To make seasoning, combine all the seasoning ingredients in a bowl. Set aside. To make butter, set red pepper in oven or toaster oven. Roast until blackened, 15 to 20 minutes. Let cool. Peel and seed. In a small bowl, mash red pepper into a purée. Add remaining butter ingredients. Whip by hand until well mixed. Set aside.

Sprinkle seasoning on a plate, enough to cover bottom. Set aside. In a small pan, melt butter over low heat. Place a fillet in the pan, flipping over to coat both sides. Set fillet into seasoning, coating both sides. Repeat for each fillet. Use more seasoning if needed. Place fillets in pan. Increase heat to high and cook until blackened on both sides and slightly crisp, 3 to 4 minutes each side. Use more butter if necessary. Serve hot with a dollop of red pepper butter.

BUILDING BLOCKS

The predominant building blocks are fruitiness from the roasted peppers and fattiness from the butter. A red wine with forward fruit works with the roasted peppers and has an oily mouthfeel that parallels the fat in butter.

FLAVORS

Choose a fruit-forward red with berry flavor to bring out the subtle flavor of fruity, roasted red pepper in the butter.

The predominant building block is fattiness from the butter, beef and pastry. A red wine with forward fruit and some fattiness has an oily mouthfeel that parallels the fat in butter, beef and pastry.

FLAVORS

Choose an older fruit-forward red that possesses some earthy tones to bring out the subtle flavor of wild mushrooms.

Mini Beef Wellingtons with Portobello Mushrooms and Thyme

SERVES 4

The mushrooms and thyme in this classic dish are subtle, but with the right wine, their flavors are drawn forth to give these Wellingtons a pleasant earthy taste.

¼ cup	50 mL	butter
4	4	beef tenderloin fillets, 1 inch (2.5 cm) thick
3	3	cloves garlic, minced
2	2	large portobello mushroom caps, finely chopped
1 Tbsp	15 mL	finely chopped fresh thyme
		salt and pepper to taste
2 Tbsp	25 mL	red wine
½	½	package frozen puff pastry sheets, thawed
1	1	egg white, lightly beaten
1 Tbsp	15 mL	butter
2 Tbsp	25 mL	all-purpose flour
1 Tbsp	15 mL	tomato paste
1 cup	250 mL	beef stock
1	1	bay leaf, crushed

In a skillet, melt 2 Tbsp (25 mL) butter over high heat and sear beef, about 3 minutes per side or until just golden. Remove beef from skillet and set aside. In same skillet, melt remaining butter and add garlic, mushrooms, thyme, salt and pepper. Stir in wine. Sauté 5 minutes, until mushrooms are tender. Set aside.

Preheat oven to 425°F (220°C). Unfold pastry sheets on a lightly floured surface and roll to ⅛-inch (0.3-cm) thickness. Cut into 4 squares. Place one fillet in center of each square, then top with mushroom mixture. Bring opposite corners of squares together over beef, gently pressing to seal. Place on a greased baking sheet and brush with egg white. Bake on the lowest oven rack 25 to 30 minutes, until pastry is golden. Keep warm.

Meanwhile, to make sauce, melt butter in a skillet over low heat. Add flour. Cook, whisking constantly, 2 to 3 minutes or until lightly browned. Add tomato paste and cook, stirring constantly, 1 to 2 minutes. Gradually whisk in stock. Season with salt and pepper. Add bay leaf and simmer 20 minutes. Pour through a wire-mesh strainer into a bowl. Serve sauce over beef Wellingtons.

Roasted Lamb Shanks
with Blackberry Sauce and Risotto

SERVES 4

Risotto is made with arborio rice that's first sautéed in butter, then boiled in broth, milk or water. The rice needs constant stirring, but it's worth the effort.

SHANKS

4	4	lamb shanks, trimmed of fat
3	3	whole peppercorns
2	2	cloves garlic, minced
1	1	bottle red wine
1	1	small onion, diced
2 Tbsp	25 mL	finely chopped fresh rosemary

BLACKBERRY SAUCE

		cooking liquid from shanks
1 Tbsp	15 mL	blackberry preserve
		salt and pepper to taste

RISOTTO

2 ½ cups	375 mL	chicken stock
½ cup	125 mL	olive oil
½	½	small onion, finely chopped
2	2	cloves garlic, minced
1 cup	250 mL	arborio rice

Place the shanks in a glass casserole dish and add remaining shank ingredients. Cover and refrigerate at least 2 hours, up to 24 hours.

Preheat oven to 350°F (180°C). Roast shanks, covered, for 2 hours. Pour off cooking liquid into a pan. Continue roasting, uncovered, another 45 minutes, until meat is very tender, about to fall from the bone. Lower heat 200°F (95°C) and keep warm.

To make sauce, boil the cooking liquid. Stir in preserve. Reduce heat and simmer until reduced and thick, 15 to 20 minutes. Season with salt and pepper. Keep warm.

Meanwhile, to make risotto, in a pot, bring stock to a boil. In a large, heavy pot, heat oil over medium heat. Add onion. Stir in garlic and rice, coating rice with oil. Make sure rice is very hot. Slowly add about ¼ cup (50 mL) stock, stirring constantly until stock is absorbed. Continue adding stock until rice is firm to bite and risotto is creamy, 15 to 20 minutes. Stir in one more ladle of stock before transferring risotto to plates. Serve lamb on risotto. Drizzle with blackberry sauce.

BUILDING BLOCKS

The predominant building blocks are fruitiness from the blackberry sauce and fattiness from the lamb and oil. A red wine with forward fruit and some fattiness works with the blackberry sauce and has an oily mouthfeel that parallels the fat in lamb and oil.

FLAVORS

Choose a fruit-forward red with lots of prominent blackberry flavor to match the flavor in the sauce.

FRUIT-BASED
SAUCES AND WINE

Dry wines can work with fruit-based sauces, but the art of this pairing can be a tricky one. Make sure the sauce contains other harmonious ingredients for the wine — such as vegetable, chicken or beef stock — and season the dish with sufficient salt. Salt helps neutralize the sweetness.

When making a fruit-based sauce, use fruit sparingly. For example, if you want to add a berry preserve, add only 1 Tbsp (15 mL). Any more than this will take the sauce from fruity to sweet. Before adding fruit to a sauce, cut into small pieces to disperse the sugar. Then, once the sauce is finished, strain out the fruit. This leaves the fruity flavor without the concentration of sugar.

CHAPTER **15**

AUSTERE REDS

PREDOMINANT BUILDING BLOCKS

- *Fattiness and bitterness with subtle fruitiness and sourness*

FLAVORS

- *Smoky, earthy, woody, coffee, chocolate, leathery, tobacco, blueberry, blackberry, raspberry, blackcurrant, cassis, tea, eucalyptus*

Austere red wines are dense, deep in color, heavy in tannin (bitterness and astringency) and high in alcohol (oily mouthfeel). While austere reds can taste bitter, the astringency occurs as chalky, grainy or silky on the palate. Wines falling into this style come primarily from New World regions, such as Australia, Chile and South Africa, but also some Old World regions, such as France and Italy.

The factors that determine wines that fall into this style are the grape variety, the geography, climate and soil conditions of the wine region, and the winemaking techniques employed. Austere reds tend to be made from red grapes with thicker skins grown in warmer climates, where the grapes can ripen fully and gain plenty of sugar. During fermentation, this sugar is transformed into alcohol, producing higher-alcohol wines.

Cabernet Sauvignon grapes, often vinified to produce austere red wine, are smaller berries with thick skins. They need less skin contact during fermentation to gain color, tannin and flavor. The juice is often fermented and aged in oak casks, which gives the resulting wines even more complexity and added structure.

Most austere reds can be matched to high-fat foods, such as chicken, duck and beef. They also can be paired to dishes containing bitter ingredients, such as olives, wild rice, red cargo rice, bulgar, radicchio, walnuts and fresh herbs, such as rosemary, lavender and savory.

The regions at top right are stylistically noted for producing austere red wines.

REGIONS

CABERNET SAUVIGNON
  Chile
  South Africa
  United States (California)

OTHERS
  Baco Noir – Canada (Ontario), France
  Barbaresco – Italy (Piedmont)
  Barolo – Italy (Piedmont)
  Haut-Médoc – France (Bordeaux)
  Margaux – France (Bordeaux)
  Pauillac – France (Bordeaux)
  Pinotage – South Africa
  Saint-Estèphe – France (Bordeaux)
  Saint-Julien – France (Bordeaux)
  Shiraz – Australia

HARMONY CHART

Cabernet Sauvignon

FOOD AFFINITIES

SEAFOOD	MEAT POULTRY	HERBS SPICES	SAUCES	CHEESE NUTS	VEGETABLES FRUITS PASTAS GRAINS
Halibut	Bacon	Black pepper	Meat stock reduction	Blue	Belgian endive
Salmon	Beef	Fenugreek	Red wine	Camembert	Black chanterelles
Tuna (rare)	Duck	Garlic	Soy	Cheddar (old)	Carrots
	Foie gras	Juniper	Walnut	Chèvre (aged)	Eggplant
	Lamb	Lavender		Parmesan	Oil-cured olives
	Sausage	Mustard		Provolone (aged)	Pasta (spinach)
	Squab	Rosemary		Walnuts	Polenta
	Venison	Savory			Red char
	Wild pheasant	Star anise			Rice (red cargo, wild)
		Szechuan pepper			Risotto
		Thyme			Summer squash

FOOD CHALLENGES

SEAFOOD	MEAT POULTRY	HERBS SPICES	SAUCES	CHEESE NUTS	VEGETABLES FRUITS PASTAS GRAINS
Anchovies	Pheasant	Chilies	Citrus	Brie (young)	Most fruit
Oysters (raw and cooked)	Pork	Cilantro	Cream	Cream cheese	Artichokes
Sardines	Veal		Vinaigrette	Swiss	Asparagus
Smoked fish					Corn
					Snow peas

BEST METHODS OF PREPARATION
Braising, grilling, roasting

BEST SEASONS
Fall, winter

COMPLEMENTARY CUISINES
French, Italian, North American

IDEAL OCCASIONS
Holidays, formal dinner, sitting by the fireplace

Celery and Blue Cheese Salad

SERVES 4

This salad is for blue-cheese lovers who like to drink red wine with their salad.

10	**10**	tender celery ribs, preferably from the interior, trimmed

DRESSING

½ cup	**125 mL**	crumbled strong blue cheese
¼ cup	**50 mL**	half-and-half cream (or as needed)
1 tsp	**5 mL**	balsamic vinegar reduction
		freshly ground white pepper to taste

Slice each celery rib crosswise into thin half moon–shaped pieces, about ¼-inch (0.5-cm) thick. Place pieces in a large bowl and set aside. To make dressing, in a food processor or blender, blend half the blue cheese and rest of the dressing ingredients until smooth. Fold in remaining blue cheese. To serve, pour dressing over the celery and toss to coat.

BUILDING BLOCKS

The predominant building block is fattiness from the blue cheese and cream and saltiness from the piquant blue cheese. An austere red wine with fattiness and bitterness works. The saltiness harmonizes with the bitterness.

FLAVORS

Choose an austere red with deep earthy flavor to match the strong, earthy flavor of blue cheese.

Olive-Crusted Red Snapper

SERVES 4

I developed this recipe to prove that big, bitter, austere reds can work with fish if the right bitter ingredients are used. The olive flavor bridges the gap between fish and heavy red wine.

½ cup	**125 mL**	each chopped green olives and chopped black olives
2 Tbsp	**25 mL**	olive oil
1 Tbsp	**15 mL**	garlic powder
1 tsp	**5 mL**	dried oregano
		salt and pepper to taste
½ cup	**125 mL**	dry breadcrumbs
4	**4**	red snapper fillets
		lemon wedges (for garnish)

Preheat oven to 450°F (230°C). In a food processor or blender, purée green olives, black olives, olive oil, garlic powder, oregano, salt and pepper to a thick paste. Transfer to a bowl. Stir in breadcrumbs. Place fillets on a baking sheet sprayed with non-stick cooking spray. Spread paste evenly over fillets, pressing firmly to coat. Bake 12 minutes or until fish is flaky and crust is golden. Serve with lemon wedges.

BUILDING BLOCKS

The predominant building blocks are subtle fattiness from the oil and bitterness from the olive crust. An austere red wine with fattiness and bitterness works.

FLAVORS

Choose an austere red with earthy, herbal flavors to match the herbal flavor of the oregano.

BUILDING BLOCKS

The predominant building blocks are fattiness from the calabrese and blue cheese and bitterness from the olive tapenade. An austere red wine with fattiness and bitterness works.

FLAVORS

Choose an austere red with bitterness to match the bitterness of the olives and transform the pungent flavor of blue cheese to a more subtle, earthy flavor with creamy texture.

Mild Calabrese and Olive Tapenade Pizza

SERVES 4

Tapenade is a thick paste made from such ingredients as olives and garlic, capers, anchovies, olive oil, lemon juice and seasonings. While it's often served as a spread, here it's a base for a delicious pizza.

OLIVE TAPENADE (CAN BE MADE ONE DAY IN ADVANCE)

3 to 4	3 to 4	cloves garlic, minced
½ cup	125 mL	each pitted black olives and olive oil
1 tsp	5 mL	dried parsley
		salt and pepper to taste
1	1	pizza crust, parcooked (see page 126)
½	½	small onion, sliced
½ lb	250 g	thinly sliced mild calabrese
½ cup	125 mL	crumbled blue cheese (or grated Parmesan)

Preheat oven to 350°F (180°C). In a food processor or blender, blend garlic, olives, olive oil and parsley until smooth. Add more oil if needed. Season with salt and pepper. Place pizza stone in oven and sprinkle with cornmeal. Spread tapenade on pizza crust. (Leftover tapenade can be refrigerated for up to 2 months.) Arrange slices of onion and calabrese over tapenade. Sprinkle with cheese. Place pizza on pizza stone and bake for 10 to 15 minutes, until crust is golden. Serve hot.

PIZZA AND WINE

The wonderful thing about pairing wine to pizza is that everything goes! The simplest approach is to consider first the cheese topping. After all, it's often the most flavorful ingredient, save for anchovies. These topping combinations and matching wine styles will get you started.

TOPPING COMBINATIONS	WINE STYLE
Tomatoes, zucchini, eggplant, chèvre, feta	Crisp, dry white
Wild mushrooms, smoked mozzarella, smoked provolone	Big, fat white
Pineapple, chicken, mozzarella	Off-dry white or off-dry rosé
Mushrooms, ripened brie	Light, fruity red
Roasted tomato, mozzarella	Red with forward fruit
Blue cheese, Parmesan, Asiago, red meat	Austere red

Risotto with Radicchio

SERVES 4

This is a simple, pleasant and classic Italian dish. The heat of the risotto slightly wilts the radicchio, leaving a hint of crispness that contrasts nicely with the risotto's creamy texture.

4 cups	1 L	chicken stock
2 Tbsp	25 mL	olive oil
1 cup	250 mL	finely chopped onion
2	2	cloves garlic, minced
1 1/2 cups	375 mL	arborio rice
1/2 cup	125 mL	dry white wine
2 cups	500 mL	finely chopped radicchio
3/4 cup	175 mL	freshly grated Parmesan cheese
1 Tbsp	15 mL	finely chopped fresh thyme
		salt and freshly ground white pepper to taste
		Parmesan (as needed)

To make risotto, in a pot, bring stock to a boil. In a large, heavy pot, heat oil over medium heat. Add onion. Stir in garlic and rice, coating rice with oil. Make sure rice is very hot. Slowly add about 1/4 cup (50 mL) stock, stirring constantly until stock is absorbed. Add wine. Continue adding stock until rice is firm to bite and risotto is creamy, 15 to 20 minutes. Stir in one more ladle of stock. Fold in radicchio, Parmesan and thyme. Season with salt and pepper. Transfer to plates. Grate Parmesan on risotto and serve hot.

BUILDING BLOCKS

The predominant building blocks are fattiness from the oil and cheese and bitterness from the radicchio. An austere red wine with fattiness and bitterness works.

FLAVORS

Choose an austere red with earthy notes to match the earthy flavor of Parmesan.

BUILDING BLOCKS

The predominant building blocks are fattiness from the veal and bitterness from the walnuts. An austere red wine with fattiness and bitterness works.

FLAVORS

Choose an austere red with earthy flavor to match the nutty flavor of walnuts and gamey flavor of this flesh.

Osso Buco with Toasted Walnut Gremolata

SERVES 4

Gremolata is the garnish sprinkled over this traditional Italian dish. Trim fat from the veal shanks; otherwise, they're too fatty and detract from the elegance of this dish.

2 Tbsp	25 mL	olive oil
4	4	large veal shanks, trimmed of fat
		flour seasoned with salt and pepper (for dredging)
4	4	large cloves garlic, chopped
1	1	large onion, diced
6	6	fresh basil leaves, finely chopped
2	2	large tomatoes, diced
1 cup	250 mL	beef stock
1 cup	250 mL	red wine
½ tsp	2 mL	grated lemon peel

GREMOLATA

½ cup	125 mL	parsley leaves
½ cup	125 mL	walnuts, toasted
		zest of 1 lemon
		kosher salt and freshly ground black pepper to taste
		garlic toast

In a large skillet, heat oil over medium heat. Dredge shanks in flour mixture. Shake off excess. Place shanks in skillet and sear until golden and crispy, about 5 minutes per side. Remove from skillet. Set aside.

Add garlic and onion to skillet and sauté until tender, about 4 minutes. Return shanks to skillet. Add basil, tomatoes, stock, wine and lemon peel. Partially cover skillet. Simmer over low heat for about 2 hours, until shanks are falling off the bone.

Meanwhile, to make gremolata, in a bowl, combine all the gremolata ingredients. Transfer veal mixture to a very large serving bowl. Sprinkle with gremolata. Serve hot with garlic toast. Use small forks to pull marrow out of shank bone to spread on garlic toast.

Bacon-Wrapped Roasted Duck

SERVES 4

This is the kind of dish that pleases protein advocates. While it's high in fat, it's fairly low in carbohydrates, making it a favorable recipe for low-carb fans.

3	3	cloves garlic, minced
1	1	stalk celery, diced
1	1	egg
½	½	small onion, finely chopped
3 cups	750 mL	cubed, dried bread
½ cup	125 mL	water
¼ cup	50 mL	melted butter
1 tsp	5 mL	each dried sage, dried oregano, seasoning salt and black pepper
1	1	duck (5 lb/2.2 kg), rinsed and dried
4	4	slices applewood smoked bacon

Preheat oven to 325°F (160°C). In a large bowl, mix together all ingredients except for duck and bacon. If too dry, add more water. Stuff dressing in duck cavity. Wrap duck in bacon strips, holding in place with toothpicks. Place duck in a roasting pan. Roast, uncovered, for about 1 ½ hours, until duck is golden and cooked inside. Let sit 10 minutes before removing stuffing and carving.

BUILDING BLOCKS

The predominant building block is fattiness from the duck and bacon. An austere red wine with fattiness works.

FLAVORS

Choose an austere red with some smoky flavor to match the smoky flavor of bacon.

The predominant building blocks are fattiness from the beef and pastry and bitterness from the tapenade. An austere red wine with fattiness and bitterness works.

FLAVORS

Choose an austere red with earthy flavor to work with the garlic and olive flavors in the tapenade.

BUILDING BLOCKS

The predominant building blocks are fattiness from the steak and bitterness from the arugula. An austere red wine with fattiness and bitterness works.

FLAVORS

Choose an austere red with smoky flavor to match the smoky flavor of grilled meat.

Beef Wellington Stuffed with Olive Tapenade

SERVES 4

After developing the Mild Calabrese and Olive Tapenade Pizza (page 154), I used the leftover tapenade to develop this recipe. The olive stuffing adds a new dimension to the beef and red wine pairing.

4	4	center-cut beef tenderloin medallions, trimmed of all fat
		pepper to taste
1 Tbsp	15 mL	olive oil
1 lb	500 g	frozen puff pastry
1	1	batch Olive Tapenade (see page 154)

Preheat oven to 425°F (220°C). Cut a 2-inch (5-cm) pocket in the center of each medallion. Season with pepper. In a large frying pan, heat oil over high heat. Sear medallions on each side until crisp, about 3 minutes per side. Let cool.

Roll out pastry into a rectangle large enough to enclose the beef. Spread with a generous layer of tapenade, place the beef on top and spoon a bit of tapenade on the beef. Wrap pastry to enclose the beef and tapenade. Repeat for remaining medallions. Refrigerate at least 15 minutes. Place on a baking sheet sprayed with non-stick cooking spray. Place in oven and immediately lower heat to 350°F (180°C). Bake for about 20 minutes, until pastry is golden.

Grilled T-Bone Steaks Drizzled with Arugula Oil

SERVES 4

Arugula is a highly aromatic salad green that works well with olive oil. Its bitterness is a natural complement to red meat.

1 cup	250 mL	packed arugula leaves, washed and dried
2/3 cup	150 mL	olive oil
		salt and pepper to taste
4	4	T-bone steaks

In a food processor or blender, purée arugula leaves, olive oil, salt and pepper. Grill steaks to desired doneness. Serve hot drizzled with arugula oil.

Steaks with Green Olive Provençal

SERVES 4

Provençal is a style of cooking celebrated in Provence, France, where olives, olive oil and garlic are staples in the diet.

4	4	beef tenderloin steaks
2 Tbsp	25 mL	olive oil
2	2	bay leaves, finely crushed
½ cup	125 mL	water
½ cup	125 mL	pitted, chopped green olives
		salt and pepper to taste
1 cup	250 mL	red wine
1	1	bay leaf
3 Tbsp	45 mL	tomato paste

Rub steaks with 1 Tbsp (15 mL) olive oil. Sprinkle with crushed bay leaves. Place steaks in glass baking dish. Cover and refrigerate 2 to 4 hours. In a saucepan, bring water to a boil. Add olives and boil for 2 minutes. Drain. Set olives aside.

Scrape most of bay leaves from steaks. Season steaks with salt and pepper. In a large skillet, heat remaining olive oil over medium-high heat. Fry steaks to desired doneness, about 4 minutes per side for medium-rare. Wrap in foil to keep warm.

Meanwhile, add wine to skillet and bring to boil, scraping up browned bits. Add olives, bay leaf and tomato paste. Reduce heat to low and simmer until thickened, stirring frequently, about 10 minutes. In a food processor or blender, purée sauce. Return to skillet. Add steaks and heat through. Serve steaks with sauce.

BUILDING BLOCKS

The predominant building blocks are fattiness from the steak and bitterness from the olives. An austere red wine with fattiness and bitterness works.

FLAVORS

Choose an austere red harmonizing with the flavors in the wine used in this recipe. Because the wine is reduced, its acidity is eliminated, leaving only the wine flavor.

BUILDING BLOCKS

The predominant building block is fattiness from the blue cheese and steak. An austere red wine with fattiness works.

FLAVORS

Choose an austere red with berry fruit flavor to work with the flavor of blue cheese.

Grilled New Yorkers with Roasted Garlic and Blue Cheese Pâté

SERVES 4

My husband is a huge fan of garlic and blue cheese, so I developed this recipe to incorporate both. This is a highly flavorful pâté, in desperate need of a powerfully flavored wine.

1	**1**	bulb garlic, skin on
1/4 cup	**50 mL**	each crumbled aged blue cheese and cream cheese
1/2 tsp	**2 mL**	dried savory or thyme
		salt and pepper to taste
		olive oil (as needed)
4	**4**	New York strip loins

Preheat oven to 350°F (180°C). In a toaster oven or oven, roast garlic until skin is black and cloves are soft. Let cool. Remove skin. In a food processor or blender, combine roasted garlic, blue cheese, cream cheese, savory, salt and pepper. Add enough oil to make mixture smooth. Transfer to a bowl.

Grill steaks to almost desired doneness. Place in a baking dish and add a large dollop of pâté on each. Transfer to oven. Heat until pâté begins to melt, 5 to 10 minutes. Serve immediately.

BUILDING BLOCKS

The predominant building blocks are fattiness from the steak and bitterness from the cocoa and coffee. An austere red wine with fattiness and bitterness works.

FLAVORS

Choose an aged austere red possessing chocolate-like or tobacco flavors to partner to the flavor of cocoa.

Ancho Coffee Dry Rub for Steak

SERVES 4

This is a great rub to seal in the moisture of steaks. Its bitterness makes it ideal to marry to red wines. You can change the amounts of coffee, chili and cocoa to suit your taste.

RUB

1/4 cup	**50 mL**	each brown sugar, unsweetened cocoa, fine-grind espresso coffee and salt
2 Tbsp	**25 mL**	each ancho chili powder or dried pepper flakes and ground black pepper
4	**4**	steaks of choice

Mix all rub ingredients together. Coat steaks generously with rub. Discard leftover rub. Cover steaks with plastic wrap and refrigerate overnight. Searing steaks first, grill to desired doneness.

DRY RUBS AND WINE

Dry rubs on grilled meats add and seal in flavors. Most are made from a base ingredient of either salt or sugar or a combination of both. Both saltiness and sweetness as building blocks in food are easily paired with wine.

Rubs can be applied to flesh just before cooking or the night before. If left for 24 hours, the rub acts like a "cure" for the flesh. To apply a rub, cut shallow slashes in the flesh and vigorously rub the mixture into the flesh.

Here are some combinations that are sure to please.

BASE INGREDIENT	ETHNIC STYLE	DRIED INGREDIENTS	FLESH	WINE STYLE
Salt	East Indian	Salt, coriander, ground ginger, turmeric, cumin, paprika, cardamom, garlic powder	Chicken	Crisp, dry white
Salt	Mediterranean	Seasoning salt, lemon pepper, garlic powder, basil	Chicken, fish	Crisp, dry white
Salt	French Provençal	Salt, rosemary, thyme, white pepper, allspice, juniper berries	Chicken, ribs	Red with forward fruit
Salt	Tex-Mex	Chili powder, cumin, onion salt, garlic salt, oregano	Ribs, beef	Austere red
Salt	Spicy Cajun	Salt, paprika, onion powder, thyme, oregano, black pepper, cayenne	Chicken	Off-dry white
Salt	Spicy Creole	Salt, paprika, white pepper, oregano, thyme, celery seeds, onion powder, garlic powder, cayenne	Chicken, beef, ribs	Off-dry rosé
Salt and sugar	Jamaican	Salt, sugar, allspice, thyme, curry powder, paprika, black pepper, nutmeg, cinnamon, ground cloves	Chicken, pork, beef, ribs	Off-dry rosé
Salt and sugar	Tennessee	Salt, sugar, black pepper, paprika, garlic powder, chili powder, onion powder, dried mustard	Chicken, pork, beef, ribs	Off-dry rosé
Salt and sugar	Spicy Moroccan	Salt, sugar, paprika, black pepper, ground ginger, cardamom, cumin, fenugreek, ground cloves, cinnamon, allspice, cayenne	Chicken, pork, beef, ribs	Off-dry rosé

CHAPTER 16

LATE HARVEST
AND **ICEWINES**

PREDOMINANT BUILDING BLOCKS

- *Balance of sourness, fruitiness and sweetness*

FLAVORS

- *Lychee, melon, grapefruit, pear, apple, mango, banana, raisin, fig, honey, vanilla*

Late harvest grapes are generally left on the vine until October. The extra time on the vine increases sugar, matures the acids and concentrates the flavors. The sugar level in the grapes determines the harvest date.

The factors that determine wines that fall into this style are the grape variety, the geography, climate and soil conditions of the wine region, and the winemaking techniques employed. Botrytis-affected (B.A.) wine is one type of late harvest wine. It has a unique bouquet and flavors reminiscent of dried fruit and honey. Under certain environmental conditions, a fungus called *botrytis cinerea*, also called noble rot, affects certain grape varieties. The botrytis fungus absorbs water from inside the grape, causing the grape to shrivel. Sugar and acid are concentrated but balanced.

In Germany, TBA wines are composed of grapes that have attained the highest stage of botrytis infection. This results in them being like raisins and, as such, these grapes give little juice during pressing. These rare wines can be cellared for years to reach their full glory.

Icewine is an intensely sweet dessert wine produced from grapes left to freeze on the vine at 17.6°F (-8°C) or lower under a cloak of protective netting. Through the fall, the grapes attain full ripeness, sweetness and flavor. During the winter, the grapes freeze and thaw, causing them to alter their chemical composition and create a unique taste. Harvested at night or on extremely cold days, the grapes are gently pressed while frozen. The ice crystals remain solid, so the only liquid to flow from the grapes is delicate nectar intensely flavored with natural sugar and a good backbone of acidity. This nectar is expertly guided through fermentation to achieve the rich and alluring qualities that make icewine.

The regions in the sidebar are stylistically noted for producing late harvest and icewines.

REGIONS

LATE HARVEST VIDAL
Canada (Ontario)

LATE HARVEST RIESLING
Canada (British Columbia, Ontario)

ICEWINES
Gewürztraminer – Canada (Ontario)
Eiswein – Germany
Riesling – Canada (Ontario), Germany
Vidal – Canada (Ontario)

OTHER SWEET WHITE DESSERT WINES
Auslese – Germany
Barsac – France
Beerenauslese (B.A.-affected) – Germany
Monbazillac – France
Moscato Passito di Pantelleria – Italy
Muscat de Beaumes-de-Venise (fortified) – France
Sauternes – France
Tokaji Aszú – Hungary
Trockenbeerenauslese (TBA, late harvest and B.A.-affected) – Germany
Vin Santo – Italy

HARMONY CHART

Riesling Icewine

FOOD AFFINITIES

SEAFOOD	MEAT POULTRY	HERBS SPICES	SAUCES	CHEESE NUTS	VEGETABLES FRUITS PASTAS GRAINS
Lobster	Duck liver	Allspice	Citrus	Most cheeses	Apples
Sole	Foie gras	Cardamom	Crème anglaise		Clementines
		Cassia	Custard		Figs
		Cinnamon	East Indian curry		Kiwi
		Cloves	Honey		Lychee
		Cumin	Maple syrup		Mangoes
		Five-spice powder	Sabayon		Melons
		Garam masala	Thai curry		Papayas
		Ginger	Tropical		Pears
		Loomi			Pink grapefruit
		Mint			Plums
		Nutmeg			Polenta desserts
					Raisins
					Sweet potato desserts
					Tangerines
					Winter squash desserts

FOOD CHALLENGES

SEAFOOD	MEAT POULTRY	HERBS SPICES	SAUCES	CHEESE NUTS	VEGETABLES FRUITS PASTAS GRAINS
Oysters (raw)	Beef	Capers	Red wine	Herb cheeses	Artichokes
	Venison	Dill	Vinaigrette		Asparagus

BEST METHODS OF PREPARATION
Baking

COMPLEMENTARY CUISINES
Spicy and hot and spicy Indian and Thai curries

BEST SEASONS
Late fall, winter

IDEAL OCCASIONS
Thanksgiving, winter holidays

ICEWINE FLAVOUR WHEEL

The Icewine Flavour Wheel allows you to articulate the particular aromas and flavors of icewine. The yin-yang color symbol within the circle represents the two primary taste sensations found in quality icewine — refreshing acidity (green) and intense sweetness (gold).

If icewine is too acidic (sour), it may detract from its concentrated fruitiness. If it's too sweet, it results in a cloying sensation that again potentially thwarts the experience of this delicious fruity nectar. Yet when acidity and sweetness are equal in intensity and harmonize as one on the palate, you know you're experiencing an authentic, excellent icewine. This balance between refreshing acidity and intense sweetness is represented by the fluidity of the yin-yang line.

The inner circle provides general terms to describe icewine, such as fruity, floral and spicy. The middle circle includes more specific terms, such as citrus, tropical or pitted fruit. The outer circle names specific fruits, such as lychee, apricot or figs. The more you use your imagination and creativity when describing the aromas or bouquet and tastes and flavors, the more fun you'll have in choosing icewines for your recipes.

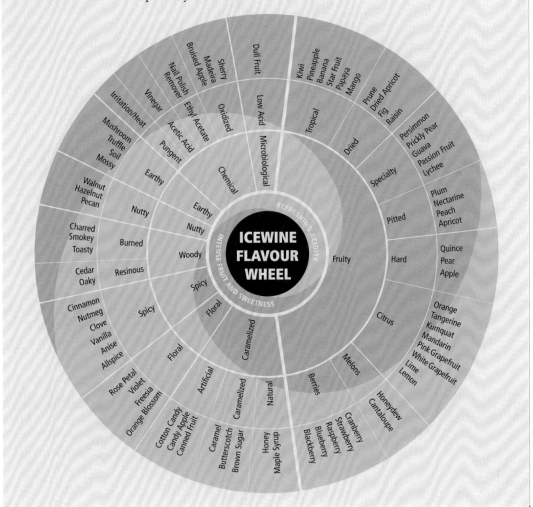

The predominant building blocks are sourness, fruitiness and sweetness from the lemon, grapefruit and melon. An icewine possessing a balance of sourness, fruitiness and sweetness is a great match.

FLAVORS

Choose a vidal icewine with lychee and melon flavors to match the flavor of the melon.

Cold Melon and Icewine Soup with Cream Cheese

SERVES 4

Chef Jean-Claude Belmont created the original version. I've changed a few ingredients to make the dish less expensive.

½	½	each honeydew melon and cantaloupe, peeled and diced
		juice of 1 ½ pink grapefruits
		juice of ½ lemon
1 ½ cups	375 mL	icewine
½ cup	125 mL	cream cheese
1 Tbsp	15 mL	sour cream
		mint leaves (for garnish)

In a food processor or blender, purée fruit. Add grapefruit juice, lemon juice and icewine and blend. Cover and refrigerate for 4 hours. In a small bowl, blend cream cheese and sour cream. Refrigerate for 2 hours. Ladle soup into cold soup bowls. Spoon a dollop of cheese mixture onto soup. Garnish with mint leaves.

Apple, Almond and Riesling Tart with Polenta Crust

SERVES 4

This is my rendition of a recipe originally created by my friend and mentor chef, Mary Evely. Mary's sense of wine and food combining is exceptional.

CRUST

¼ cup	50 mL	butter, softened
2 Tbsp	25 mL	brown sugar
1	1	egg, room temperature
1 ½ cups	375 mL	all-purpose flour (as needed)
½ cup	125 mL	polenta
½ cup	125 mL	ground almond
pinch	pinch	salt

FILLING

6	6	cooking apples, peeled and cored
		juice from 1 lemon
¼ cup	50 mL	Riesling wine jelly*

*Apricot or orange jelly can be substituted.

Preheat oven to 350°F (180°C). To make crust, in a bowl, cream together butter and sugar. Add egg, 1 cup (250 mL) flour, polenta, ground almond, salt. Knead very gently, adding more flour to make dough dry if needed. Wrap in plastic wrap and refrigerate for 15 minutes.

On a lightly floured work surface, roll out dough in a rectangle large enough to fit into a baking sheet. Spray sheet with non-stick cooking spray. Place dough on sheet and parbake 8 to 10 minutes.

Meanwhile, slice apple into rings and place in a bowl, being careful not to break them. Drizzle lemon juice over rings. Pour wine jelly into bowl. Coat apples with jelly. Lay apple rings on the crust, overlapping in a decorative manner. Bake tart 30 to 40 minutes, until apples are cooked and crust is golden. Cool slightly before serving.

BUILDING BLOCKS

The predominant building blocks are sourness, fruitiness and sweetness from the apples and Riesling wine jelly. An icewine possessing a balance of sourness, fruitiness and sweetness is a great match.

FLAVORS

Choose a Riesling icewine with apple-pear flavors to match the apple flavor.

Apricot Galette

SERVES 4

"Galette" is French for a round, flat cake made of pastry dough. In this recipe, I've used puff pasty. Its richness works nicely with the rich, intense flavors of a late harvest wine.

¼ cup	50 mL	sliced almonds
2 Tbsp	25 mL	icing sugar
6	6	fresh underripe apricots
½	½	package frozen puff pastry sheets
1 Tbsp	15 mL	granulated sugar
		clotted cream (for garnish)

Preheat oven to 425°F (220°C). In a food processor, pulse almonds with icing sugar until finely ground. Pit apricots and cut into wedges ⅛ inch (0.3 cm) thick. On a lightly floured surface, unfold pastry sheet and cut out a 9-inch (23-cm) round. Transfer round to a buttered large shallow baking pan and prick pastry all over with a fork.

Spoon almond mixture evenly over pastry, leaving a ¼-inch (0.5-cm) border. Decoratively arrange apricot wedges, overlapping them, on top of almond mixture. Sprinkle with granulated sugar. Bake on middle rack until edges are golden brown, about 30 minutes. With a metal spatula, transfer galette to a rack to cool for 5 minutes. Serve pieces with a dollop of clotted cream.

Individual Vanilla Custards with Fresh Melon

SERVES 4

The custard's creamy texture, along with the melon's soft sweetness, enhances the icewine's concentrated flavors and richness.

1	1	plump moist vanilla bean, split lengthwise
1 cup	250 mL	whole milk
2	2	large egg yolks
1 Tbsp	15 mL	dark maple syrup
		boiling water (as needed)
½	½	honeydew melon

Preheat oven to 325°F (160°C). Cut a piece of waxed paper to line a baking pan large enough to hold 4 ramekins. Cut 3 slits in the waxed paper and line the pan. Place the ramekins in the pan and set aside.

In a medium saucepan, combine the vanilla bean and milk over high heat. Bring to a boil and remove from heat. Cover and set aside to meld for 15 minutes. In the bowl of an electric mixer, whisk the egg yolks and maple syrup until thick and lemon-colored. Set aside.

Bring the vanilla-infused milk back to a boil and very gradually add to the yolk mixture in a thin stream, whisking constantly. Let stand 2 to 3 minutes, then remove any foam that has risen to the top. Divide the mixture evenly among the ramekins. Pour enough boiling water into the pan to reach about halfway up the ramekins. Cover pan loosely with foil.

Bake on middle rack until the custards are just set at the edges but still trembling in the center, 30 to 35 minutes. Carefully remove ramekins from pan. Refrigerate, loosely covered, for at least 2 hours, up to 24 hours. Peel and slice melon and serve with custard.

BUILDING BLOCKS

The predominant building blocks are fruitiness and sweetness from the melon and maple syrup. An icewine with fruitiness, sourness and sweetness is a match.

FLAVORS

Choose a vidal icewine with pineapple and melon flavors to match the flavor of melon.

BUILDING BLOCKS

The predominant building blocks are fruitiness and sweetness from the mango and kiwi. An icewine possessing a balance of sourness, fruitiness and sweetness is a great match.

FLAVORS

Choose a vidal icewine with mango, pineapple or kiwi flavors to match the mango and kiwi flavors.

Buttermilk Panna Cotta with Mango and Kiwi

SERVES 4

"Panna cotta" is Italian for a lightly textured and lightly flavored custard. Make this the day before you intend to serve it.

2 Tbsp	25 mL	water
2 tsp	10 mL	plain gelatin
1 cup	250 mL	whipping cream
2 cups	500 mL	buttermilk
¾ tsp	4 mL	vanilla extract
2	2	mangoes
4	4	kiwi

Pour the water into a small custard cup and sprinkle gelatin over. Let stand until gelatin softens, approximately 10 minutes. In a saucepan, stir whipping cream over low heat until it melts, then immediately remove from heat. Stir in gelatin mixture until it's completely dissolved and mixture is smooth. Cool cream mixture to room temperature, about 45 minutes. Stir in buttermilk and vanilla. Divide mixture evenly among four ramekins. Refrigerate until panna cotta is set, about 24 hours.

Run a thin, sharp knife around sides of each ramekin to loosen. Place a ramekin in 1 inch (2.5 cm) of hot water for 30 seconds. Immediately invert onto plate. Using both hands, firmly grasp ramekin and plate together, shaking gently to settle panna cotta. Repeat for each. Peel and cube mango and kiwi. Spoon fresh fruit mixture around each panna cotta and serve.

Fresh Fig and Grape Frangipane Tart

SERVES 4

You can freeze the dough for the tart shell for up to 1 month. The frozen dough is as easy to work with as fresh.

TART SHELL

1 cup	250 mL	soft butter
3/4 cup	175 mL	icing sugar
2 cups	500 mL	flour
2 Tbsp	25 mL	vanilla extract
pinch	pinch	salt

FRANGIPANE

1 cup	250 mL	butter, unsalted, at room temperature
1 cup	250 mL	almond powder
1/4 cup	50 mL	granulated sugar
3	3	eggs
3 Tbsp	45 mL	flour
1 tsp	5 mL	vanilla extract
1/2 cup	125 mL	halved fresh figs
1/2 cup	125 mL	quartered grapes

To make tart shell, in a large bowl, combine butter and icing sugar. Mix with fork until fluffy. Add flour, vanilla and salt. Mix with fork until crumbly. Do not overmix. Pull dough together into a ball. Wrap in plastic wrap and refrigerate for 1 hour. Press dough into a 8- x 4-inch (1.5-L) loaf pan with a removable bottom. Trim dough flush with edge of pan. Refrigerate for 30 minutes. Preheat oven to 375°F (190°C). Line tart with parchment paper and weight down with dried beans. Bake until golden, about 15 minutes. Remove parchment paper. Let cool.

To make frangipane, in a stainless steel bowl, cream butter with almond powder and sugar. Add the eggs one at a time, whisking constantly. Sift flour over the bowl and fold gently. Add the vanilla and mix gently.

Fill the tart shell with frangipane mixture to three-quarters full and smooth with a spatula. Arrange figs and grapes on top, pressing gently. Bake until frangipane is golden, about 40 to 45 minutes. Let cool completely before serving.

BUILDING BLOCKS

The predominant building blocks are fruitiness and sweetness from the figs and grapes. An icewine possessing a balance of sourness, fruitiness and sweetness is a great match.

FLAVORS

Choose a vidal icewine with dried fruit flavors to match the flavors of figs and grapes.

BUILDING BLOCKS

The predominant building blocks are fruitiness and sweetness from the grilled apples, pears and ice cream. A late-harvest wine with a balance of sourness, fruitiness and sweetness is a great match.

FLAVORS

Choose a late harvest riesling with apple or pear flavor to match the fruit.

Maple-Glazed Apples and Pears on Vanilla Ice Cream

SERVES 4

Other fruits can be used in this dessert. Just pair the prominent fruit flavors of the wine you'll be serving with any complementary fruit firm enough to be sliced into rings.

2	**2**	apples, cored, peeled and sliced into 2-inch (5-cm) rings
2	**2**	pears, cored, peeled and sliced into 2-inch (5-cm) rings
		juice from 1 lemon
2 Tbsp	**25 mL**	dark maple syrup
		vanilla ice cream (as desired)

Put apple and pear slices in a bowl and drizzle with lemon juice. Add maple syrup and toss, coating fruit slices. Grill on high heat until golden, 2 to 3 minutes per side. Serve hot over vanilla ice cream.

Mango Chimichangas

SERVES 4

This dish can take on an Asian slant by using dampened rice paper instead of tortillas. Rice paper is more delicate-tasting, allowing the mango to be the most predominant flavor.

⅓ cup	75 mL	ground almonds
6	6	ripe mangoes, peeled and diced
		juice of 2 limes
2 tsp	10 mL	soft butter
4	4	thin 7-inch (18-cm) flour tortillas
		vegetable oil (for deep-frying)
		icing sugar (as needed)
		clotted cream (for garnish)

Preheat oven to 350°F (180°C). Sprinkle ground almonds on a baking sheet. Bake until toasted, 2 to 3 minutes. Let cool. In a saucepan, bring mangoes and lime juice to a boil. Reduce heat to low and simmer until mixture is very thick, about 5 minutes. Stir in the butter and almonds until butter is melted. Set mixture aside to cool, about half an hour.

Spoon a quarter of mango mixture into the center of a tortilla. Fold the sides in, then roll up tightly, securing the chimichanga with toothpicks. Repeat with the remaining fruit and tortillas. Pour at least 3 inches (8 cm) oil in a heavy, deep skillet. Heat until almost smoking. Fry the chimichangas, one or two at a time, turning, until light golden, 3 to 4 minutes. Drain and sprinkle with icing sugar shaken through a sieve. Serve immediately, topped with clotted cream.

BUILDING BLOCKS

The predominant building blocks are fruitiness and sweetness from the mango. An icewine possessing a balance of sourness, fruitiness and sweetness is a great match.

FLAVORS

Choose a vidal icewine with tropical flavors to match the mango flavor.

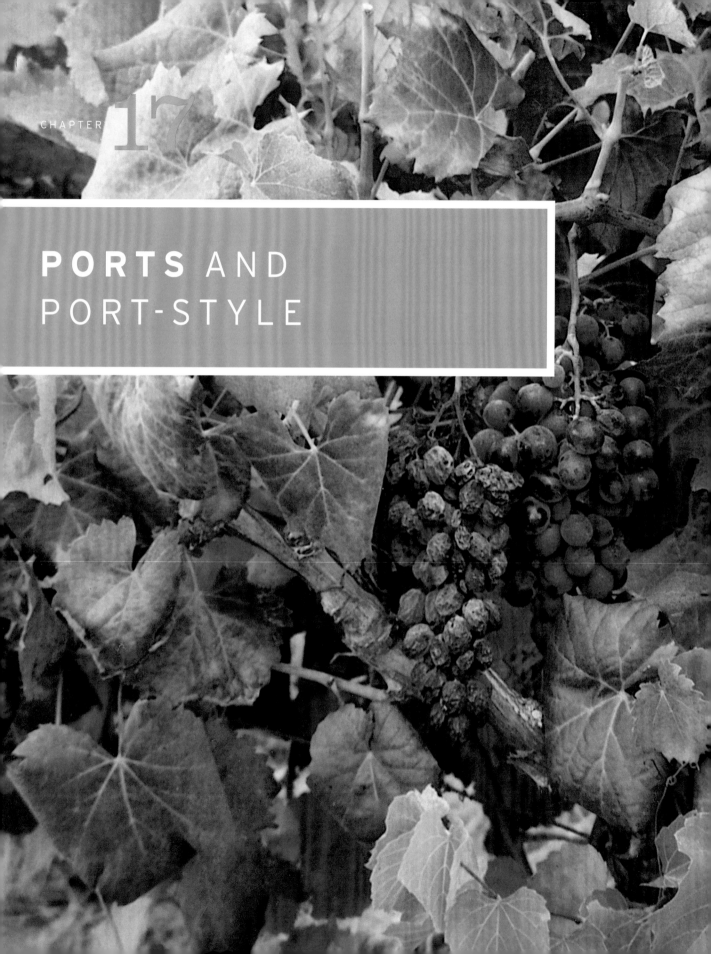

CHAPTER 17

PORTS AND PORT-STYLE

PREDOMINANT BUILDING BLOCKS

- *Fruitiness and sourness in dry Port or dry port-style wines*
- *Fruitiness and sweetness with some bitterness in sweet Port or sweet port-style wines*

FLAVORS

- *Nutty, toasty, smoky, spicy caramelized, woody, chocolate, hazelnut, raisin, plum and prune*

This wine style includes both authentic Port, produced only in Portugal, and port-style wines, produced all over the world. Both are fortified, which means brandy is added to the wine. Each brand adds its own character and distinctiveness, along with higher alcohol.

In terms of sweetness, Port can be very sweet, sweet, semi-dry, dry or extra dry. The winemaker determines the sweetness. During fermentation, the sugar levels in the wine are monitored. When about half of the grape sugar has been turned into alcohol, the wine is run off into a larger vat or barrels containing brandy (traditionally one part brandy to four parts wine). The brandy instantly halts the fermentation.

The fortified wine is then shipped downstream to the Port shipper's lodges in the coastal town of Vila Nova de Gaia. At the lodges, the Port is sampled and classified according to style, sweetness and color. The quality Ports are left to age for over a year. After this time, some are selected to be Vintage Port while the others are blended. The final versions are submitted to the Instituto do Vinho do Port, the governmental authority that analyzes and guarantees a Port's authenticity. If approved the Port receives a certificate of origin and guarantee seal.

Port is loosely divided into two categories: wood-aged and bottle-aged. Wood-aged Ports are matured in oak and ready to drink when bottled. Wood-aged Ports include white Port, ruby Port (tinto aloirado) and tawny Port (aloirado). Bottle-aged Ports are left to mature in the bottle, thus protected from the air. They include Vintage Port, Single Quinta Vintage Port, Port Wine with the Date of Harvest, Crusted or Vintage-Character Port and Late Bottled Vintage Port (LBV).

The following regions are stylistically noted for producing Port or port-style wines.

REGIONS

PORT – PORTUGAL
Crusted
LBV
Ruby
Single Quinta
Tawny
10-year-old tawny
20-, 30- and
   40-year-old tawny
Vintage
White

OTHERS
Mavrodaphne of Patras
   – Greece
Muscadel – South Africa
Port-style – Australia, Canada
   (British Columbia, Ontario),
   New Zealand, United States
   (California)

HARMONY CHART

Tawny Port-Style

FOOD AFFINITIES

SEAFOOD	MEAT POULTRY	HERBS SPICES	SAUCES	CHEESE NUTS	VEGETABLES FRUITS PASTAS GRAINS
Most seafood	Duck	Aleppo peppers	Coffee	Almonds (toasted)	Dried fruit
	Goose	Caramel	Crème brûlée	Cheddar	Onions (caramelized)
	Pâté (duck, pork)	Cassia	Dried fruit	Gorgonzola	Risotto desserts
	Venison	Chocolate (dark)	Mexican mole	Mascarpone	Sweet potato desserts
		Cinnamon	Port	Ricotta	Winter squash
		Fennel	Port and mushroom	Roquefort	Winter squash desserts
		Fenugreek	Sabayon	Stilton	
		Five-spice powder		Walnuts (roasted)	
		Garam masala			
		Juniper berries			
		Lavender			
		Mint			
		Nutmeg			
		Panch phoron			
		Spearmint			
		Star anise			
		Turmeric			

BEST METHODS OF PREPARATION
Making of desserts, sauces

COMPLEMENTARY CUISINES
Dark chocolate-based desserts

BEST SEASONS
Winter

IDEAL OCCASIONS
By the fireplace, holiday get-together, skiing day

FOOD CHALLENGES

SEAFOOD	HERBS SPICES	SAUCES	CHEESE NUTS	VEGETABLES FRUITS PASTAS GRAINS
All fish	Capers	Citrus	Chèvre	Artichokes
Shellfish	Chives	Mayonnaise	Feta	Asparagus
	Cilantro	Sour cream	Parmesan	
	Coriander	Vinaigrette	Quark	
MEAT POULTRY	Cumin	Yogurt		
	Garlic			
Chicken	Grains of paradise			
	Green cardamom			
	Kaffir lime leaves			
	Lemon grass			

Venison Steaks in Port and Orange Reduction

SERVES 4

Due to its gamey flavor, venison requires more seasoning and spice than beef. It is considered fat free and so is drier in texture, which means it can easily be overcooked.

15	15	juniper berries, roughly crushed
		zest from 1 orange (reserve orange juice)
1 tsp	5 mL	cinnamon
		sea salt and freshly ground black pepper to taste
2 Tbsp	25 mL	sunflower oil
4	4	venison steaks
10	10	pitted prunes, soaked in 1/2 cup (125 mL) boiled water
3/4 cup	175 mL	tawny Port
1/4 cup	50 mL	butter

In a mortar and pestle or small blender or food processor, crush together juniper berries, orange zest, cinnamon, salt and pepper. Season steaks with spices. Cover and refrigerate for 4 hours.

In a frying pan, heat oil over medium heat. Fry steaks for 3 to 4 minutes per side. Remove from pan. Wrap in foil and keep warm. Remove prunes from water and reserve water. Chop prunes coarsely.

Add prunes, prune water, reserved orange juice and port to the hot frying pan, scraping the bottom to mix in any sediment. Bring to a boil and whisk in butter. Simmer over low heat until sauce is reduced and thick, 7 to 10 minutes. Season with salt and pepper if necessary. Pour sauce on plates. Serve steaks over sauce.

BUILDING BLOCKS

The predominant building blocks are fruitiness and sweetness from the berries, prunes, orange juice and Port. A Port or port-style wine with fruitiness and sweetness is ideal.

FLAVORS

Choose a tawny Port or port-style wine possessing raisin and prune flavors to work with the prunes.

The predominant building blocks are fruitiness and sweetness from the apples, sugar and Port. A Port or port-style wine with fruitiness and sweetness is ideal.

FLAVORS

Choose a white Port or port-style wine with sweetness and nutty flavor to work with the flavor of apples.

BUILDING BLOCKS

The predominant building blocks are sweetness and bitterness from the dark chocolate and walnuts. A Port or port-style wine with sweetness and a hint of bitterness is ideal.

FLAVORS

Choose a tawny Port or port-style wine with chocolate and caramel flavors to work with the chocolate and walnut flavors.

Port-Flamed Apple Sabayon

SERVES 4

Sometimes the easiest recipes are the tastiest. Here's one.

SABAYON

4	4	medium egg yolks
1 Tbsp	15 mL	caster sugar
1 Tbsp	15 mL	white Port
¼ cup	50 mL	butter
1 tsp	5 mL	caster sugar
2	2	apples, peeled, cored and cut into rings
1 Tbsp	15 mL	white Port

To make sabayon, in a bowl over simmering water, whisk in egg yolks and sugar. Stir until thick and creamy. Remove bowl from heat and stir in Port. Cover to keep warm. In a medium sauté pan, melt butter and sugar over low heat. Add the apple rings and fry until golden and soft. Add the white Port and flambé, tilting the pan away from you. Cook off the alcohol for 1 to 2 minutes. Set apple rings on plates and drizzle with sabayon.

Dark Chocolate and Walnut Torte

SERVES 4

After several attempts, I finally found the right measurements and ingredients to have this wonderful torte work with a port-style wine.

½ cup	125 mL	chopped walnuts
3 Tbsp	45 mL	butter
6	6	squares semi-sweet chocolate
3	3	eggs, beaten
1 cup	250 mL	clotted cream
½ tsp	2 mL	vanilla extract
1	1	parbaked pie shell

Preheat oven to 350°F (180°C). Sprinkle walnuts on a baking sheet. Bake until toasted, 4 to 5 minutes. Let cool. In a medium saucepan, melt butter over low heat. Add chocolate, stirring constantly until smooth. Fold in eggs and cream. Remove from heat. Stir in walnuts and vanilla. Pour mixture into pie shell. Bake 40 to 45 minutes, until center is set. Serve warm or chilled.

Chocolate and Chèvre Truffle Cake

SERVES 4

The original version of this recipe was created by chef Alex Begbie. I've reworked it to pair with a Port or port-style wine.

RASPBERRY SAUCE

1 cup	250 mL	fresh raspberries
2 Tbsp	25 mL	sugar
		vegetable oil for greasing pan (as needed)

CAKE

1 lb	500 g	Belgian semi-sweet chocolate
½ lb	250 g	butter
¼ lb	125 g	fresh chèvre
6	6	eggs
½ cup	125 mL	fresh raspberries
		condensed cream (for garnish)

To make raspberry sauce, in a saucepan, bring raspberries and sugar to a boil, stirring occasionally. Let cool. Strain sauce through a sieve. Cover and chill 2 to 3 hours.

To make cake, in the top of a double boiler set over simmering water, melt chocolate and butter. Beat in chèvre until well mixed. Transfer to a bowl. In the cleaned top of the double boiler set over simmering water, beat eggs with a hand mixer until light and fluffy and tripled in volume. Fold into chocolate mixture, blending well.

Preheat oven to 425°F (220°C). Line the sides and bottom of an 8-inch (2-L) springform pan with parchment paper. Grease the parchment paper with vegetable oil. Pour in half the batter. Sprinkle with raspberries, then pour in remaining batter. Smooth top with a spoon. Set springform pan into shallow pan, then half fill with warm water. Bake 5 minutes. Cover with a sheet of buttered foil. Do not let foil touch top of cake. Bake another 10 minutes. Let cool for 3 hours before removing sides. Cake will firm as it cools. Serve at room temperature with a pool of raspberry sauce and a generous dollop of cream.

BUILDING BLOCKS

The predominant building blocks are sweetness from the raspberries, sugar and cream and bitterness from the semi-sweet chocolate. A Port or port-style wine with sweetness and a hint of bitterness is ideal.

FLAVORS

Choose a ruby Port or port-style wine with berry flavors to work with the raspberry flavor.

CHOCOLATE AND WINE

Use dark chocolate when pairing with wine. Milk chocolate has very little cocoa and lots of sugar and oil, making it too sweet. When pairing dark chocolate to red wine, the predominant building block in wine to consider is bitterness. Austere reds have enough to partner well with semi-sweet or unsweetened dark chocolate.

If serving sweeter dark chocolate (such as North American dark chocolate), choose a wine that has sweetness as its predominant building block. For example, red Ports and red port-style wines work extremely well with dark chocolate. The chocolate is less sweet than the sweetness in this style of wine, making for a harmonious combination.

BUILDING BLOCKS

The predominant building blocks are sweetness and bitterness from the bittersweet chocolate. A Port or port-style wine with sweetness and a hint of bitterness is ideal.

FLAVORS

Choose a tawny Port or port-style wine with lots of chocolate and nutty flavors to work with the bittersweet chocolate flavor in this cake.

Unadulterated Chocolate Cake

SERVES 4

Jen Bird, who runs the catering company Unforgettable Edibles, created this recipe. Make the cake the night before, giving it time to set. It's scrumptious!

1 lb	**500 g**	Belgian bittersweet chocolate, in pieces
½ lb	**250 g**	butter, cubed
8	**8**	whole eggs, cold

Preheat oven to 325°F (160°C). In a non-stick saucepan, melt chocolate and butter over low heat, stirring often. Pour into a bowl. Beat eggs with electric mixer on high for 5 minutes, until doubled in size. Fold one-third of egg mixture into chocolate mixture until very few streaks remain. Repeat for remaining egg mixture, gently stirring until no streaks remain.

Line a 9-inch (2.5-L) springform pan with parchment paper and grease the sides. Pour batter into pan. Place in a larger baking pan and fill with boiling water until it just covers the larger pan's bottom. Bake 25 to 30 minutes, until top is just cracking and glossy (like a brownie). Cool completely before serving.

Blue Cheese, Pecan and Maple Syrup Bundles

SERVES 4

One day, my wine- and food-loving friend Lisa Alguire told me she had "just the best recipe." She was right. It's easy and delicious and works with both Port and port-style wines.

2	2	sheets frozen phyllo pastry, thawed in refrigerator overnight
¾ cup	175 mL	crumbled blue cheese
1 Tbsp	15 mL	ground pecans
2 Tbsp	25 mL	dark maple syrup
		melted butter (as needed)

In bowl, combine blue cheese, pecans and maple syrup. Cover and refrigerate for 1 hour. Preheat oven to 350°F (180°C). Unroll pastry and cover with a damp towel. Lay out one sheet of pastry. Brush with melted butter. Lay the other sheet of pastry on top. Brush with melted butter.

Cut pastry into 9 squares. Place a heaping tablespoon of blue cheese mixture in center of each square. Fold the corners of pastry into the middle and pinch closed at the top. Place bundles on a baking sheet sprayed with non-stick cooking spray. Bake 10 to 15 minutes, until pastry is golden.

BUILDING BLOCKS

The predominant building block is sweetness from the maple syrup. A Port or port-style wine with sweetness is ideal.

FLAVORS

Choose a white Port or port-style wine with nutty flavors to match the flavor of pecans, while working with the piquant flavor of blue cheese.

INDEX

M

macadamias, pairing with wine, 87
maceration, carbonic, 129
Malbec, 139
malolactic fermentation, 63, 77
mangoes
    Baked Ripened Brie with Mango, 102
    Buttermilk Panna Cotta with
      Mango and Kiwi, 170
    buying, 102
    Grilled Halibut with Mango-Ginger
      Sauce, 110
    Lobster and Mango Salad, 102
    Mango Chimichangas, 173
    Spicy, Crispy Trout Soup with
      Green Mango, 132
Manicotti with Roasted Tomato-Garlic
  Sauce, 146
maple syrup
    Blue Cheese, Pecan and Maple
      Syrup Bundles, 181
    Cured Ham with Maple Syrup and
      Apple Glaze, 104
    Maple-Glazed Apples and Pears on
      Vanilla Ice Cream, 172
    Orange Roughy with Lemon-
      Maple Butter Sauce, 105
    Roasted Winter Squash Risotto
      with Maple Syrup, 111
maps, tongue, 13–14
Margaux, 151
Marinated Chèvre with Sun-Dried
  Tomatoes and Roasted Garlic, 38
Marinated Shrimp with Hoisin-Lemon
  Dipping Sauce, 107
Mateus Rosé, 115
Mavrodaphne of Patras, 175
Mayan Hot and Sour Chicken Soup, 97
mayonnaise
    Cumin-Polenta Crusted Pork Loin
      with Chipotle Mayonnaise,
      124
    Grilled Chicken on Focaccia with
      Garlic-Parsley Mayo, 88
    Mediterranean Crab Cakes with
      Chipotle Mayonnaise, 121
    Saigon Burgers with Lime-Jalapeño
      Mayonnaise on a Baguette, 106
meatballs
    Chinese Rice-Studded Meatballs
      with Lime Dipping Sauce, 39
    Hazel's Meatballs, 124–25
Mediterranean style
    Cold Mediterranean Pasta Salad,
      52–53
    Mediterranean Crab Cakes with
      Chipotle Mayonnaise, 121
    Rotini Mediterranean, 59
medium-bodied whites. *see* well-balanced,
  medium-bodied, smooth whites
medium-tasters, 12–13
melons
    Cold Melon and Icewine Soup with

    Cream Cheese, 166
    Individual Vanilla Custards with
      Fresh Melon, 169
    Rolled Prosciutto and Melon with
      Burrini, 42
Merlot, 139
Meursault, 77
Mexican style
    Central American Chicken in
      Almond Sauce, 73
    Tex-Mex Turkey Burgers with Corn
      Salsa, 60
Mild Calabrese and Olive Tapenade
  Pizza, 154
Mini Beef Wellingtons with Portobello
  Mushrooms and Thyme, 148
mint
    Rack of Lamb with Mint Pesto, 145
Monbazillac, 163
mood, effect on wine tasting, 28
Moscato Passito di Pantelleria, 163
mozzarella
    Mozzarella and Roasted Red
      Pepper Bruschetta, 141
    Tuscan White Bean Bruschetta, 65
muenster
    Pork Rouladen with Muenster, 89
Müller-Thurgau, 95
Muscadel, 175
Muscadet, 47
Muscat de Beaumes-de-Venise, 163
mushrooms
    Mini Beef Wellingtons with
      Portobello Mushrooms and
      Thyme, 148
    Potato Galettes with Wild
      Mushrooms and Thyme, 84
    Rigatoni with Baby Portobello
      Mushrooms and Toasted
      Pistachios, 87
    Ripened Brie and Rosemary
      Bruschetta, 142
    Wild Mushroom and Barley
      Risotto, 143
mussels
    buying and cleaning, 81
    Seafood Salad with Feta and Lemon
      Vinaigrette, 55
    Soup of Mussels, Leeks and Fresh
      Chervil, 81
must, 129

N

Napa cabbage, described, 106
New Yorkers
    Grilled New Yorkers with Roasted
      Garlic and Blue Cheese Pâté, 160
Noble, Ann, 25
noble rot, 163
non-tasters, 12–13
noodles
    Asian Pasta Salad with Grilled
      Jumbo Shrimp, 58

    Cold Buckwheat Noodles with
      Thai Basil Vinaigrette, 57
    pairing with soy sauces (and wine),
      107
Notes, wine, described, 7
nuts. *see also specific nuts*
    pairing with wine, 87

O

oak barrel aging, 77
off-dry rosés, 115, 129
    complementary recipes, 117–27
    described, 115
    Harmony Chart, 116
off-dry whites
    complementary recipes, 97–113
    described, 95
    Riesling Harmony Chart, 96
oka
    Oka and Summer Sausage
      Pancakes, 91
    Velouté Soup of Fiddleheads and
      Oka, 69
olfaction, 11
olfactory epithelium, 24
olive oil
    Beef Wellington Stuffed with Olive
      Tapenade, 158
    Grilled T-Bone Steaks Drizzled
      with Arugula Oil, 158
    Wild Rice and Bulgar Salad with
      Lemon, Garlic and Olive Oil, 44
olives
    Beef Wellington Stuffed with Olive
      Tapenade, 158
    Cold Mediterranean Pasta Salad, 52
    Mild Calabrese and Olive Tapenade
      Pizza, 154
    Mozzarella and Roasted Red
      Pepper Bruschetta, 141
    Olive-Crusted Red Snapper, 153
    Racks of Lamb with Four Cheeses,
      93
    Rotini Mediterranean, 59
    Steaks with Green Olive Provençal,
      159
    Wild Rice and Bulgar Salad with
      Lemon, Garlic and Olive Oil, 44
onions
    Caramelized Onion, Chèvre and
      Walnut Pizza, 126
    Onion and Bacon Tart, 68
    Onion Parcels of Smoked Salmon
      and Cream Cheese with Chives,
      50
Orange Roughy with Lemon-Maple
  Butter Sauce, 105
oranges
    Venison Steaks in Port and Orange
      Reduction, 177
Original Greek, 38, 43
ortho-nasal olfaction, 11
Orvieto, 47